earth
future

earth
earth
future

Stories from a Sustainable World

Guy Dauncey

NEW SOCIETY PUBLISHERS

Cataloguing in Publication Data:

A catalogue record for this publication is available from the National Library of Canada.

Cover design by Miriam MacPhail.

Book and page layout by Jeremy Drought

Printed in Canada on acid-free, partially recycled (20 percent post-consumer) paper, using soy-based inks by Transcontinental/Best Book Manufacturers.

New Society Publishers acknowledges the financial support of the Government of Canada through the Book Publishing Industry Development Program (BPIDP) for our publishing activities, and the assistance of the Province of British Columbia through the British Columbia Arts Council.

Paperback ISBN: 0-86571-407-X

Inquiries regarding requests to reprint all or part of *Earthfuture: Stories from a Sustainable World* should be addressed to New Society Publishers at the address below.

To order directly from the publishers, please add $4.00 shipping to the price of the first copy, and $1.00 for each additional copy (plus GST in Canada). Send check or money order to:

New Society Publishers

P.O. Box 189, Gabriola Island, British Columbia, V0R 1X0, Canada

New Society Publishers aims to publish books for fundamental social change through nonviolent action. We focus especially on sustainable living, progressive leadership, and educational and parenting resources. Our full list of books can be browsed on the worldwide web at http://www.newsociety.com

NEW SOCIETY PUBLISHERS

Gabriola Island, British Columbia, Canada

Contents

Preface

Today, something is happening to the whole structure of human consciousness. A fresh kind of life is starting. Driven by the forces of love, the fragments of the world are seeking each other, so that the world may come into being.
Pierre Teilhard de Chardin

Archimedes, speaking of the power of the lever, is supposed to have said, "Give me but one firm spot on which to stand, and I will move the world." Today, we say, "Give us a vision big enough, and the courage to act, and we will change the world."

These short stories are offered as a vision of the world's future as an ecologically sustainable, just society, in which we are able to work our way through the many challenges that confront us. The stories are not about the completion of the vision, but the making of the vision, the process by which we summon up the hope and the determination to make it happen.

Someone once said that an optimist is someone who hasn't understood all the facts. That may be true — but it is also true that a pessimist is someone who hasn't understood all the opportunities. The models, the technologies and the human motivations that we need to create a paradise on Earth already exist.

Around the world today, there is a blossoming of initiative, creativity and personal commitment by people who have the determination to make this world a better place. The skills and the experience, we pick up along the way. It is these people who are the role-models for my stories — which is another way of saying that almost all of the initiatives described in the stories *are already happening*, as the notes explain. They are a celebration of the present, projected into the future.

*Never doubt that a small group of thoughtful, concerned citizens
can change the world. Indeed, it is the only thing that ever has.*
Margaret Mead

Some readers might think that the stories are unrealistic, because they
ignore the many barriers that stand in their way. The biggest of these
barriers, however, is the belief that the barriers are insurmountable — and
this we have the power to remove, because it exists in our own minds. We
need to be outrageous in our visions, and steadfast in our belief that our
visions can come true. We are like molecules in an amazing parade, about to
form an organism. We CAN build a solar society. We CAN stop the tiger from
becoming extinct. We CAN close down the World Trade Organization or the
World Bank, if that is what it takes. It IS possible: the biggest enemy is not
the global corporations or the banks; it is our own willingness to become
cynical, instead of being outrageously vibrant in pursuit of our dreams.

It's like taking the wave in surfing. The wave is the dream, which we
can ride to a different future. So hold tight to your dreams, and remember
the fourth law of sustainability: "If it's not fun, it's not sustainable."

• • •

I would like to thank my wonderful wife, Carolyn Herriot, for her
patience and support while I was writing this book, and brewing an earlier
version, and my sister, Jane Dauncey, for her practical encouragement and
support. I would also like to thank Robbie Andersen, Sandi Ayer, Dolores
Broten, Martin Burger, Andy Caffrey, Michael Clague, Roger Colwill, Ross
Crockford, Caspar Davis, Duane Elgin, Bill Holloway, Terence Hughes,
Nancy Field, Lori Kmeck, Rich Mably, Michael Mascall, Kathryn Molloy, Don
Poole, Janit Rabinovitch, Bill and Jackie Robson, Rhys Roth, Mike Simpson,
Tonia Rushall, Al Rycroft, Dave Shishkoff, Rob Squires, Coro Strandberg,
Bruce Torrie, the Grameen Foundation and many others, for their
encouragement and assistance (and some for their patience in reading

through an earlier unpublished version of the book, which was written as a novel). I would also like to thank my publishers, Chris and Judith Plant, for their courage to test the water with this new approach to social-change publishing, and Audrey McClellan for her invaluable editing.

If you want to keep up to date with the kinds of positive initiatives described in these stories, I recommend *YES! Magazine* (PO Box 10818, Bainbridge Island, WA 98110, USA. yes@futurenet.org).

My home is just outside the city of Victoria, on Vancouver Island, on Canada's West Coast, which is why several of the stories are set on the island. We *all* need to create visions for our homelands, to invent the futures that we want to inhabit. I would like to see films, even musicals, set in the possible future. If you have written a story set in the future about your neighborhood, region or country, which expresses the values of human compassion, social justice and ecological sustainability, and you would like see your story listed at my website, e-mail it to me at guydauncey@earthfuture.com. I'll set up a link to your home page, and New Society Publishers will consider publishing the best.

This book has a website at **www.earthfuture.com**, where you will find links to the groups and organizations that are working to realize the visions, alternative endings to *Kamchatka's Reprieve*, readers' feedback, and more. I hope you enjoy reading the stories as much as I have enjoyed writing them.

Guy Dauncey
Victoria, British Columbia
September 1999

Visit Earthfuture's website at
www.earthfuture.com

There Is Only Ourselves

There is no other person who is going to do it. There is only you and me and friends who share in the spirit. This is our planet. There is no one "out there" who is going to put the bad things right. Only ourselves.

Don't delay, then, by blaming other people or sitting at home complaining. Don't let negativity corrode your energy. It will also corrode your dreams.

The way we live now and in the future really is in our hands. We can choose to live with hope and love and inspiration. The huge collective residue of past negativity, fear and pessimism is only alive if it is alive in our hearts. It can be scattered to the winds when we choose to carry hope and vision in its place. There is only ourselves.

Going Organic

The Edge of Dartmoor, Southern England
September 2005

Jolene's back ached as she patiently gathered the seeds from the huge broccoli plants that grew next to the greenhouse. In the ten years she'd been gardening, it didn't get any easier on her back. Her friends had suggested she set up a hammock where she could take occasional breaks, but there was always so much to do. Hammocks were for lazy Sunday evenings, not workday afternoons.

It had been incredibly dry that summer all over southwestern England. By September, the reservoirs on Dartmoor were lower than anyone could recall, and the River Dart was down to a mellow trickle, the tiniest memory of last winter's stunning torrents. The water shortage had made it a difficult year for Going Organic's members, most of whom cultivated small patches of land, either in their backyards or on land leased from local farmers, without the use of chemical pesticides or fertilizers. Very few had wells, and the water board's restrictions limited them to early-morning watering, by hand, between 5 am and 7 am.

Jolene had no complaints. Being up with the dawn had given her a summer filled with beautiful memories, and a joyful intimacy with the wildlife that lived on the southern edge of Dartmoor. There was the pair of peregrine falcons who hunted for their breakfast of mice and rabbits at that time of the day; an old badger who regularly came home to the woods from wherever he'd been foraging; the myriad birds — and the skylarks, oh, the skylarks! singing their timeless praise at the break of another day. Before the paper arrived, before the telephone started ringing — those were the hours that Jolene loved the best, when as the poet William Wordsworth put it, "Bliss was it in that dawn to be alive, but to be young was very heaven!"

Wordsworth had been writing about another time, two hundred years before, when his generation had been changing the world as Jolene and her friends were today. Then, the struggle had been against feudalism and the power of the landed aristocracy. Today, it was against globalism and the power of the corporate dollarocracy, but as in Wordsworth's time, they were winning! The legal and political victories were beginning to push back the invasion of local cultures and economies by corporate tentacles, and you could feel the optimism in the air as news of the various victories flashed around the Internet and onto people's dinner tables. Last month the World Trade Organization had reluctantly agreed to include community and environmental representatives on its various committees; and just a few days ago, Jolene had heard that the World Bank was going to be subjected to an independent audit to examine complaints that its projects undermined local economies.

Three years earlier, Jolene and her friends had launched Going Organic as a way to satisfy the growing demand for locally grown organic food while enabling local people to earn some additional income. There were several organic farms that operated local brown-box schemes, providing a weekly box of fresh fruit and vegetables to their customers, but there was a limit to how much they could grow. The other brown-box programs in the area depended on imported food, which sometimes came from as far away as France, or even California.

The idea behind Going Organic was that by pooling their produce, small growers and backyard gardeners could operate their own co-operative brown-box program, contributing to the sustainability and self-sufficiency of the region while earning some useful income. All that was required was a central storage building with cooling facilities, and a system to record what crops members would be providing each week. For Jolene, this meant checking the garden to see what was ready, logging onto the Going Organic home page on the Internet to post the information, then delivering her contribution to the depot once a week. For co-op members without Internet access, there was always a neighbor willing to extend the favor.

From the six they had started with, the scheme had grown to involve fifteen hundred growers in just three years. The only rule was that you had to grow your food organically. If your garden was not certified organic, you had to make a formal application to become an organic grower, and enter the seven-year transitional process.

It was the variety of the members that astonished Jolene. Stockbrokers and students, factory workers and artists, shopkeepers and consultants — they all enjoyed the process of growing extra food and contributing it to the community pot. Their youngest member was ten-year-old Jesse, who grew radishes, parsley and seven varieties of lettuce. Their oldest was ninety-five-year-old Brenda, whose leeks, kale and parsnips helped keep the program going in winter and whose compost was the talk of the region. And then there was Charlie, an ex-con and loner who had asked a local farmer if he could cultivate the strip of land that lay fallow along the edge of a field. He religiously brought in a sack of carrots every week, for which he received the princely sum of £20. Quite a few of the members grew food in their neighbors' gardens, maintaining the flower beds and giving them fresh produce in exchange for the use of the land. Between them, they distributed food to 17,000 local people, delivered mostly by bicycle, with their trademark aluminum towing carts.

The co-op had grown beyond their highest hopes, but this summer, because of the drought, their customers hadn't always had a full box of vegetables. The most worrying aspect of the drought was that they could no longer kid themselves that it was a one-off affair. By the normal weather patterns of the past hundred years, they should have expected one three-month drought every twenty years — not three in the past ten years. No one said "if" anymore when they talked about the frightening realities of global warming. It was still a shock, however, to accept that this might mean the end of all that was comforting and familiar. What if a dry summer like this was followed by a winter without rain, as happened in northern Spain last year? Over there, the farmers were abandoning lands their ancestors had farmed for centuries, maybe millennia. The thought that she might one day have to leave this joyful corner of paradise was a brooding maggot in Jolene's beautiful apple that kept her awake at night, especially when the moon was full. Why had we screwed up so badly, she asked herself, that we should have broken the very stability of the world's climate, and (in parts of the world) ended the biological flow of millennia? All for the thrill of driving, of unrestricted rushing along the country's lanes and motorways, pouring out the carbon emissions that were bottling up the sun's heat, slowly frying the Earth? Surely, we could not have been that foolish. To think that they had cut down whole forests and ancient woods to accommodate more cars and encourage more driving. What folly.

Today, the new laws required everyone to drive fuel-efficient hybrid cars and obliged the electric utilities to produce 25 percent of their power from renewable sources. But when you allowed for the ten-year phase-in period that industry had negotiated, the reduction in carbon dioxide emissions was minimal. For Jolene and her fellow farmers there was one unexpected benefit in the form of the carbon storage checks that they received in official acknowledgment that organic farming stored greater quantities of carbon in the soil than chemical farming. The check always came in handy just after Christmas, even if it had been paid by some oil or gas company that was using the scheme to keep on producing. It was a bit of nonsense, if you paused to think about it.

As she pondered these thoughts and gathered her broccoli seeds in the special seed pouch her mother had sewn for her, Jolene found herself overcome by an immense feeling of sadness. Locally, life seemed to be growing more and more beautiful, even if her back did still ache and her lover had been away in Sweden for the past three months. Local stewardship groups were eliminating pollution from Devon's rivers and streams, community groups were slowing the traffic on residential streets, and they had stopped the progress of genetically modified foods in its tracks when it seemed destined to take over the world. Everywhere, community initiatives were blossoming, filling the region with a wonderful freshness. People even spoke of a new renaissance. And now this. What good would these seeds be if there was no water? What good, come to that, would the land be? It was a heavy thought to bear; no wonder her back ached.

Notes

In England, full organic certification requires seven years. In Europe, there was a thirty-fold increase in organically managed land over the years 1986 to 1999. At the current rate of change, thirty percent of Europe's agriculture will be organic by the year 2010, which is astonishing the forecasters and policy gurus. In Wales, the new Welsh Assembly has set its sights on one hundred percent of the farms in Wales becoming organic. For information on organic farming in Britain, contact The Soil Association, Bristol House, 40–56 Victoria Street, Bristol, BS1 6BY, UK.

Brown-box programs (also known as Community Supported Agriculture) are taking off wherever there are organic growers. In Victoria, B.C., several brown-box programs deliver by bicycle, using specially designed aluminum carts (see **www.bikecartage.com**).

Carbon storage rebates for organic growers are not yet a reality, but they probably will be soon, since research at the Rodale Institute's experimental farm in Pennsylvania has shown that by using traditional organic soil conservation techniques, farmers can double the amount of carbon stored in their soil.

The progress of genetically modified foods in Britain ground to a halt in May 1999, when sixty percent of Britain's food distributors pledged not to stock genetically modified (GM) food on their shelves. This followed a widespread consumer revolt which had roots in south Devon, where supporters of an organic farm near Totnes tore out a genetically modified crop from the neighbor's farm for fear that it would infect the organic crops. For information on the dangers of GM food, see *Farmageddon: Food and the Culture of Biotechnology* by Brewster Kneen (New Society Publishers, 1999), and *The Ram's Horn* (monthly, $20/year from S-6, C-27, RR1, Sorrento, British Columbia, V0E 2W0, Canada; ramshorn@jetstream.net).

The fears of drought are alarmingly real, as anyone knows who lives on the east coast or the Midwest of the USA. One of global warming's key characteristics is an increase in the turbulence and unpredictability of the world's climate.

A Future in the Forest

David Bradshaw needed his morning's walk to clear his head after last night's party. He was sure that the celebrations had continued long after he had left.

He loved the forest on a Saturday morning, when the working week was behind him. The path was soft beneath his feet, and the towering fir and cedar trees had such an ancient understanding of silence, accentuated by the rough-edged call of a raven as it flew across the forest canopy. Up until yesterday, this forest was scheduled to be clearcut within five years, its beauty reduced to a few hundred trucks full of logs plus a pile of slash for burning and some badly damaged soil. Today, its future was safeguarded forever.

Dave had lived in Port Renfrew with his wife Lynn and their three children for twenty years, working at a variety of jobs in the forest and on the water. The tiny community was perched on the west coast of Vancouver Island at the end of the road from Victoria, "waiting for its future to begin," as Dave had always felt. The succession of forest companies that owned much of the town and the surrounding forest had cast a long shadow over the community, holding it captive to the past and to a distant boardroom in some downtown Vancouver office building, of which it was a colonial outpost.

He paused to watch two deer grazing together in a clearing, where an old fir tree had fallen several winters ago. It gave Dave an unfamiliar feeling of rightness to realize that these deer would never again need to abandon their territory. Nor would the cougars or the black bears or the wolves. From this day on, the forest ecosystem would be allowed to grow ever more rich, instead of being subjected to the sixty-year rhythm of abuse that the system of industrial logging demanded, until its soil was gone and it could no longer regenerate itself as a forest.

In spite of a lifetime spent working in the woods, it was only five years ago that Dave had begun to appreciate what a west coast rainforest really was, and realized that it didn't mature until some of its trees were 300 years old or more. At the age of sixty, a tree is only twelve years old, in human terms. If it is left to grow, it will put on five times as much timber in its second sixty years, and five times as much again in its third sixty years, before finally slowing down. To clearcut the forest at the age of sixty was not a smart thing to do if you wanted a steady flow of timber. How could a distant corporation understand that a forest was best left to grow, and that you should only cut its annual growth, leaving the capital intact, harvesting only the interest? A forest was a long-term ecosystem, which needed long-term economic planning, not short-term plundering. How else would his kids and grandchildren have jobs in the forest, fifty years from now?

Dave hadn't always thought like this. For fifteen years, he had been a typical west-coaster, living high on the abundance of nature. In the good years, he had pulled in $60,000 from logging and an additional $70,000 from the commercial fishing boat he operated. They worked hard and lived well, enjoying winter holidays in the Bahamas. His wife had grown up in Port Renfrew and knew almost everyone, including the people from the Pacheedaht native band, who lived on the reserves outside the village.

It was around the time that his son Andrew was eighteen, and his fourteen-year-old daughter Sunshine had been diagnosed with irritable bowel syndrome (a supposedly incurable problem), that Dave started to question what his life was all about. He began to read more, and when a group formed in Port Renfrew to explore the possibility of applying for a community forestry license in the hope of assuming greater control over the region's forests, he volunteered to join.

For some people, the instinct to learn comes late in life. Dave had left school at eighteen and gone straight to work in the forest. For fifteen years, he had lived in a culture where logging was king, where the shiny pick-up truck was queen, and where the environmentalists were the sworn enemy. Once Dave started reading and thinking for himself, however, a whole new world began to open up.

After twenty minutes, the pathway rose to the top of a ridge where he stopped to take in the view. The full grandeur of the Pacific Ocean spread out before him, with the morning fog drifting in close to the shore. The forest looking down on the water had been clearcut recently, opening up the view of the ocean.

The jobs in Port Renfrew had been terrible these past few years. Most of the sports and commercial fishermen had sold their boats because of the salmon closures, and many of his logging friends had been out of work because of the forest crisis. What was a man in his forties or fifties to do when life crumbled around him like that? Only ecotourism was thriving, as thousands came to hike the famous West Coast Trail, staying at the inn to rest and freshen up after the journey. If only they could take control of the local forests themselves, Dave and his committee began to realize, they could manage them in an ecological way, custom-mill the timber, and produce jobs for their youngsters in local spin-off businesses. Port Renfrew could begin to have a future, instead of just a past.

It often takes a generation to change the world and the way the world thinks. It starts slowly with small groups of people meeting in rooms together, organizing conferences and workshops. As the word spreads, more people join, and soon they are organizing demonstrations, lobbying ministers and writing articles in the papers. Then some of their members get themselves arrested for blockading a forest road or occupying a minister's office, until sooner or later they catch the public's spirit, and the politicians can no longer ignore them.

That is exactly what happened to forestry in British Columbia and south of the border in Washington and Oregon. The anger over the destruction of the rainforests spilled over into mass arrests, and out of the pain and confusion, a whole new vision emerged of sustainable forestry, where the woods would be managed by local communities along ecological lines, where logging, ecotourism, mushrooms, medicinal plants, recreation, habitat for fish and wildlife and the whole forest ecosystem would be equally valued.

The key to the transition lay in certification, as it did for organic food. An organization called the Forest Stewardship Council had set the standards, and all over the world, forest companies were changing their methods to receive certification, and customer approval. In Europe, from the Atlantic to the Ural Mountains, fifteen percent of the forests were now being managed according to eco-certified standards. Even the Russians were falling into line, helped by a steady market for certified timber and investments from socially responsible investors in western Europe and North America. It was the consumers who were leading the movement, refusing to buy timber which had not been managed in a sustainable manner, and channelling their investments into funds that supported eco-certified forestry.

For a while, it looked as if the World Trade Organization was going to outlaw the system by ruling that eco-certification was an impediment to global investment and free trade, but when the public found out, the uproar was so deafening that the politicians were forced to back down. It was this victory which finally persuaded the government of British Columbia to pass the Community Forest Trust Act, giving local communities the power to manage their forests for eco-certification, either independently (on Crown land) or in partnership with the larger forest landowners, coupled with a tax penalty for companies that failed to set up such partnerships. By 2010, every forest company in British Columbia would either have to make the transition to fifty-one percent community control, or be taxed heavily enough to encourage them to change their habits.

At the party last night, after the speeches celebrating the signing of the new community forest license, Dave had danced with his wife and daughter, and then with half the women in the community — Port Renfrew was that kind of place, where everyone knew each other and there was an easy sense of friendship. The excitement continued on through the dancing. There was talk of setting up a community-controlled development corporation to purchase land from the logging company and turn the rather haphazard settlement into a place they could feel proud of. There was talk of expanding the local store. There was talk of setting up a windpower co-operative to build a windfarm along the coast, producing renewable energy while keeping more of their money in the community. Everyone shared in the excitement and the feeling that their future was finally in their own hands. They had still been dancing at 11 pm when Dave left to take Sunshine home, because she said she was feeling weak.

Looking out over the glorious calm of the Pacific Ocean, Dave knew that yesterday had been a crucial turning point for the community. There was a lot of work ahead, to be sure, but they were up for it. The new millennium was looking good! Maybe someone would even find a cure for Sunshine.

Notes

There is a very real crisis in the rainforests of western Canada. The government of British Columbia has started to experiment with community forest licenses, and a *Community Forest Trust Act* is being proposed by groups such as the EcoForestry Institute and the Eco-Research Chair at the University of Victoria. Their recommendations apply to publicly owned Crown land, whereas in the story, the proposal is extended to include larger tracts of privately owned forest land. For more on the *Trust Act*, see **www.law.uvic.ca/~elp**.

Eco-certification is a critically important part of this process. By early 1998, the Forest Stewardship Council had put its seal of approval on 15.5 million acres worldwide, including Sweden (six million acres), the United States (four million acres) and Poland (four million acres). In August 1999, Home Depot (which sells ten percent of the world's timber supply) announced that it would be phasing out timber products that were not eco-certified by 2003. In 1998, IKEA, Nike, 3M Corp, IBM and Hewlett-Packard made a similar pledge. For details, see **www.fscus.org**. The newly formed International Network of Forests and Communities is a worldwide network of communities that are pursuing sustainable forestry — see **www.forestsand communities.org**.

Earth Day

Michelle woke the kids early and got them dressed for the *Fête de la Terre* that was to be held that day in the Bois de Boulogne, attended by tens of thousands. The whole day a holiday! In place of work, there would be the morning's huge Earth Parade, followed by a concert in the park and an afternoon of fun and games.

Her children, Jacques (nine), Pierre (seven) and Mathilde (six) had no trouble getting up. This was their big day. For weeks, their school had been preparing a float for the parade, representing all the different spring wildflowers that could be found in Paris. With help from *Les Amis de la Terre*, they had approached thousands of Parisians who now grew wild flower gardens, however small, and received 50,000 francs in sponsorships, which they had used to tear up their concrete playground, replacing it with a beautiful wildlife garden and a vegetable patch, with its own composting toilet.

As they joined the thousands in the parade, dancing and walking along the banks of the Seine towards the Bois, surrounded by music, balloons, bicycles and people on stilts, Michelle felt a wonderful sense of shared purpose. Why this very real sense of celebration, when just a few years ago, everything had seemed so hopeless? The fashionable attitude used to be one of intellectual cynicism. Had the world's many social and ecological crises suddenly been resolved?

Hardly so, Michelle thought, as she looked at the hats and the long-sleeved T-shirts which her children wore to protect them from the searing rays of raw sunshine that would soon be pouring through the hole in the ozone layer. Nor did the planet's food shortage make her feel particularly hopeful. With the Earth's population growing by 200,000 people a day, and

China and India importing eighty million tons of grain a year, grain prices had
doubled since 2003. Lining up to buy food coupons at the shelters for the
poor was not something she enjoyed when she had three children to feed.

But with the turning of the millennium, it felt as if something had
shifted. In villages and towns throughout France, it was as if people had
woken up and realized that if they didn't get up off their backsides and do
something, no one else would. The old idea that you could go on
complaining and expect someone else to sort out the mess seemed
suddenly dead. Cynicism was out, determination was in. And with that
shift, a wave of new energy had been released into the community.

Building on the achievements of the 1990s, Paris now boasted
hundreds of organic urban farms, encouraged by the food crisis and the
regulations against the use of chemical pesticides and herbicides. Streets
all over the city had been closed off to cars, many being ploughed up
and redesigned as winding footpaths, bicycle trails and urban gardens.
Later in the summer, apartment blocks would blossom with beans and
squash growing on trellises that climbed up their sides, and sunflowers on
their roofs.

In the realm of the economy, the Paris Fund for Economic Alternatives
was attracting thousands of new people to invest in social and ecological
businesses. Even the city's chronic problem of unemployment was getting
better, helped by the community trusts, which supported the city's
arrondisements as they developed their own local economies, using local
welfare funds to invest in personal career enhancement, small businesses
and microventures. Since 2002, the whole of France had been enjoying
a four-day week, releasing an impulse of creative leisure activities and
family events.

The average Parisian knew a lot more about global warming now. Ever
since the incredible winter of 2003, when temperatures across northern
France had plunged to -20°C and remained there for almost three weeks,
there was a much improved awareness in people's minds of the threat of
climate change. A tough system of ecological taxes discouraged people
from driving all but the most fuel-efficient cars, and towns and cities

across France had been ordered by the government to prioritize cycling and public transport over private vehicles. The far-sighted ecovillages legislation had put an abrupt end to further suburban sprawl, while encouraging the existing suburbs to develop their own local economies and village centers.

Taken in combination, these things were releasing an infectious sense of possibility that was empowering an entire generation. If these things were possible, what else might be possible? Maybe the only limits truly were in the mind. Maybe the future really could be whatever people made it to be.

As the throng of people gathered in the Bois de Boulogne for the day's celebrations, streaming in from all quarters of the city, Michelle looked around and wondered if her children would be celebrating Earth Day in fifty years, their grandchildren beside them. The problems were still so huge, and pessimism could so easily return if people surrendered their hope.

Rêvez, l'impossible rêve, a man sang from the stage, keeping alive Jacques Brel's intoxicating songs for another generation. That dream, she thought — that dream. All my life, I've worked for that dream: a world in which everyone could experience personal fulfillment, community health and ecological harmony. Should that be so very difficult, so hard to achieve? Didn't everyone share the same dream, at some deep level? And yet for years they had been so few, always trying to do too much with never enough people to do what was needed. She felt so grateful to the ones who had kept the dream alive, including those who were no more, who had crossed over. They would be so happy to see us here today, she thought, so proud of what everyone was doing.

"Regard, Maman — le ballon! Le voila! Le voila!" Mathilde cried out, as the first of a hundred hot-air balloons drifted slowly into view over Paris. "Regardez! Les ballons!" came the voices of hundreds more children, joined by the adults, followed by whistles, horns and drums. Then everyone stood up and started singing *Rêvez, l'impossible rêve*, ten thousand voices joined together in song, calling out their hopes for the world to hear.

Yes, we can do it, Michelle thought, as she felt the energy of ten thousand hearts. *Never doubt that a small group of thoughtful concerned citizens can change the world*, a small voice said inside her head, reminding her of the words of the famous American anthropologist, Margaret Mead: *Indeed, it is the only thing that ever has.*

"Yes," Michelle thought, "it is possible. We can do it, if we want to."

The Song of Syntropy

Srinagar, Kashmir, Northern India
April 2006

Iqbal Kharoun awoke before dawn, put on his kurta, and stepped outside to greet the mystery of another day. From the verandah of the bungalow where he and Elizabeth were staying in the hills of Kashmir, five miles outside Srinagar, he could see the forest on the other side of the valley dotted with flowering cherry and apricot trees, and the lake below them shrouded in mist. It was so beautiful, as if the world had just been born, and knew nothing yet of hatred, argument or cruelty.

He lay a rug across the verandah floor and settled down to meditate, folding his legs and tucking in his feet. Of all of the many places he had visited around the world in this last hectic year, there was none that could compare to this. If heaven had been allowed to settle and grow on Earth, it was here.

He closed his eyes, inhaled deeply, and observed his breath for five minutes. Then focusing on the silence within his being, he gradually entered another world where space, consciousness and stillness took on a new geography, and where the less he did, the further he traveled. It was a ritual he had followed ever since his twelfth birthday, and yet each day was a new exploration. It was good to be back in India after all his travels.

In her bed in the back of the bungalow, Elizabeth Mitchell was slowly awakening, stretching her limbs and luxuriating in the sensation of the clean white cotton sheets against her naked skin. Outside, the sky was slowly brightening, and the outline of the mountains was becoming an exotic purple as they emerged from their sleep under the night sky. It felt so darned good to be here, so good to be *alive*. Their work was going well, Iqbal's young friends were such good company — and this place was simply wild. New York was wild too, but in a different way.

Elizabeth and Iqbal had come across each other's work through the pages of the *Journal of Consciousness Research*, and had corresponded for several years, becoming friends, before finally meeting at a conference in Phoenix, Arizona, and working together to write their book, *Syntropy.* Elizabeth was twenty-eight, tall and blonde, with a confident New York style and a colorful life that could fill several biographies. Raised in the city by progressive Greek-American parents, she had majored in geography and climatology at McGill University in Montreal, and then traveled around the world from Mexico to South Africa to Hawaii doing her Ph.D. on ethno-climatology — the influence of aboriginal culture and shamanistic rituals on the climate.

She had been married twice, once to a clean-cut college kid from Vermont, and once to a Kung bushman in the Kalahari desert, which had amused his clan enormously, since she was a foot taller than he was. Among this remote tribe of bushmen, Elizabeth had discovered an undisturbed tradition, and she marveled at their ability to communicate with nature. Christian missionaries had got to most of the tribes in southern Africa a century earlier, burning their sacred drums and banning their dances, destroying a source of knowledge that was tens of thousands of years old, but the missionaries had not got to the Kung. It was among the Kung that Elizabeth started to develop her ideas about the chi-anthropic principle, which led her to link up with Iqbal.

Iqbal was twenty-six years old. He was shy, with an all-too-perfect English accent that he had picked up at Brockwood Park, a private school in Hampshire, southern England. His father was a prominent Kashmiri professor of law and ethics, his mother a French biologist, poet and mystic. It was she who had taught him how to meditate, taught him to question everything, and introduced him to the great Indian philosophers, from Sri Vivekananda and A.K. Coomaraswamy to Sri Aurobindo.

His homeland, Kashmir, had an almost mystical aura of beauty which had captivated generations before him, and continued to do so, in spite of its present conflicts. The forests, mountains and lakes were elevated to a magical, otherworldly beauty when filled with the gentle aroma of the pine trees, suffused with the fragrance of apricot, peach and plum blossoms. In the school holidays, between spending time exploring the Muslim mosques and the Buddhist monasteries, he and his mother had gone on treks into the nature reserves, where Iqbal had been astonished by the variety of species which inhabited the forests, from the snow cocks and golden orioles to the brown bears and musk deer.

The problem that Iqbal had wrestled with, amid all this beauty, was that while the science he was learning at school did an incredible job of integrating nature's myriad species into a glorious evolutionary whole, it stopped at the doorway of consciousness. The professors of physics and biology at the college in Srinagar where his father taught, knew more about molecules of moon dust than they did about the minds of their neighbors, the monks and yogis who had been studying the geography of inner space since long before the prophet Muhammad arrived, or the Buddha sat under his banyan tree.

The second law of thermodynamics said that everything within a closed system tended towards greater disorder and chaos, and yet the first (unwritten) law of meditation said quite the opposite, that everything tended towards wholeness and peace. How could it be, his sixteen-year-old mind asked, that two such enormous truths should be at odds with each other? Evolution described a world that became ever more complex and organized — so how could the scientists say that it was becoming more disorderly, that entropy reigned supreme? It was certainly true in a limited case such as Dal Lake, the jewel in the heart of Srinagar, which was becoming more putrefied with every load of sewage that was dumped into it, starving its aquatic inhabitants of oxygen and demonstrating the case for entropy with every breath they took. But that was a local breakdown of the way it *could* be. With proper stewardship and a properly built solar aquatic sewage treatment plant, the lake could be quickly restored to its former health, the sewage transformed into water lilies and rich, dark compost.

None of these thoughts rolled through Iqbal's mind as he penetrated deeper into the inner world, through the mists of memories towards the heart of oneness where everything became light, and every barrier dissolved. He had no task to achieve, no goal to pursue. He simply had to stand guard against the incursion of outer thoughts and let his mind move out of the way, allowing "The Great No-Thing" to enter.

• • •

Elizabeth was out running, exhilarating in the aroma of pine needles and peach blossoms, when she heard the cry from the path that led to their house.

"Tell Mr Iqbal — you both come quickly! Come very quickly!" the small boy shouted as soon as he saw her. "You both terrible trouble, terrible trouble, Miss Elizabeth," he panted as he reached her. "They coming for you! The police, the mullahs — they all coming! They want kill you! You hide! You run quickly!"

Elizabeth knew immediately what must have happened. She sprinted back to the house, where Iqbal had heard the shouting and was already stuffing a few things into a backpack. She rushed to her room to fill a bottle of water, grab the emergency backpack they had organized just in case, and gather up a few personal things, including her pocket computer, and the copy of *Syntropy* which had been signed by the Dalai Lama, the aging astronaut Edgar Mitchell, and the vice-president of the United States.

Moments later, with Amjad (the boy who had given the warning) they were hurrying up a hidden trail that led to the hills, and the secret places that Iqbal knew from his childhood where they could hide out until the threat subsided, or until they devised some way to escape. It was a long walk to the Ladakh Valley, and the passes through to Tibet, and safety.

A *fatwah* was a very serious matter. It was an open declaration by the fundamentalist Islamic mullahs that the book *Syntropy* had been found to be an alien doctrine that was offensive to Islam, and that anyone who killed the authors would be praised and rewarded. Who would have thought that a simple book could have caused such an uproar?

Elizabeth was always hopeful, however, and she knew that if she could send out a message that they were in trouble, a storm of protest would descend on the mullahs who had pronounced the *fatwah*, and the Indian and Pakistani leaders who had allowed it to be spoken.

They set a swift pace, and after an hour, they paused to drink and catch their breath. The views from the mountainside were spectacular, and the path behind them seemed silent and empty. Without a lookout, however, they had no means of knowing whether their pursuers were following. It was fortunate that the Srinagar police did not use dogs, out of an old prejudice that dogs were lower creatures, and unclean.

"I know a place where there's fresh water, where they'll never find us," Iqbal said. "We'll be there by mid-day, if we keep going. It's got a good lookout, which would give us an hour's lead if we saw them coming. It's so silly. Do they think they can stop the whole of evolution? To think that two of the largest religious traditions in the world, the Muslims and the Christians, both ancient enemies, are combining forces to try to prevent people from discussing a new idea. It's not silly — it's hilarious!"

"It's also dangerous," Elizabeth replied. "And I, for one, want to go on evolving a bit longer, rather than finish my life as the target of an assassin's bullet. I've got a *huge* amount of living planned for the next fifty years. As soon as we get to your hideaway, I'll set up my solar array and start sending messages to tell the world what's happening. I doubt that they'll think to block the satellites."

"Ah, Elizabeth. I do admire you. You have such a wonderful spirit. I sit in meditation every day for hours, inviting the invisible world to fill me, while in you, it just blazes out everywhere. You must be cautious, however. I am not the only child of Srinagar who grew up in these hills and knows the secret pathways. They may even be able to track your signals."

"Come on then — let's go!" Elizabeth replied, and they plunged back into the forest undergrowth.

· · ·

When Iqbal Kharoun and Elizabeth Mitchell's book, *Syntropy*, was published in 2005, the scientific world had responded with a storm of protest and delight. To some, their work represented the most exciting breakthrough in scientific thinking since Einstein's work on relativity a hundred years before. Others compared them to Galileo, or Copernicus. In a feature review, *TIME Magazine* said:

> The implications of syntropy theory for science, and the cosmological foundations on which science has been based since the seventeenth century, are nothing short of stupendous. We have entered a new era of human knowledge and discovery.

For more traditional scientists, however, the theory was more than they could handle. The editor of *The Journal of Biological Sciences* wrote:

> This mixing of religious foofaraw with the rigor of science has produced a bastard, a mish mash of new-age beliefs masquerading as science. Scientifically speaking, Kharoun and Mitchell's work is as good a candidate for burning as any we have seen.

Christianity Today was quick to join in with its own brand of judgment:

> This [syntropy] demonstrates the danger of meddling in the works of God. The leaders of the scientific community must take care not to endorse every piece of crackpot new-age nonsense that appears. The time has come for responsible Christians to stand up and say "Enough!" We should render unto God that which is God's, and unto science that which is science's. Science has no business meddling in the affairs of God.

The theory which was causing such a stir stemmed from Iqbal's realization that science's rigorous separation of the physical world of matter and energy from the spiritual world of consciousness was nothing more than a device the early-seventeenth-century scientists had employed to give themselves some breathing space, and to protect themselves from being burned at the stake by some witch-hunter or grand inquisitor from the Catholic Church. It was a messy business, with its preliminary stages of imprisonment and torture, before the victim was dragged to a market square, tied to a stake and burned alive, inch by painful inch.

The burning was a problem for people like Galileo, who had started looking at the universe through a telescope to see what was actually there, instead of taking the word of the priests as final. To the early scientists, the meticulous process of observing, measuring, deducing and testing different hypotheses was proving to be a very powerful method of advancing their knowledge about the natural world. The church, however, did not like to have people disagreeing with or questioning its pronouncements. It had a frightening arsenal of torture and death to deal with such people.

It was in response to this arsenal that the French philosopher René Descartes had proposed a new method, declaring that the world consisted of two separate but linked realities, *res mens* (things of the mind) and *res extensa* (things extended in space). The church could say what it wanted about res mens, but the scientists would focus their energies solely on *res extensa*, where the truth could be determined by careful observation and measurement, not by the presumptions of paranoid priests.

The implications of the new method were profound. Slowly at first, and then with increasing speed, it liberated people from the morass of fears and superstitions which had kept them in darkness and made them hang onto ancient beliefs. The light of reason poured in, displacing the gloomy recesses of the medieval age and leading to discoveries and inventions that the twenty-first century took for granted: gravity, space stations, nanotechnology.

Descartes' new method did not deny the place of God, or spirit. In his mind, the two realms existed side-by-side, like a married couple who had stopped speaking to each other but still lived together in the same house. As the years went by, however, the husband exiled his wife to the basement, and then covered the trap-door with a mat. He began to deny the existence of the spiritual world, and the silence people pray to as God.

The universe became a place of energy and matter, out of which life had sprung by the haphazard chemistry of chance. For a professional scientist to dabble in things of the spirit brought scorn, and the risk of dismissal. It wasn't as cruel as incineration, but it was just as effective.

For Iqbal, this exile of all things spiritual was bewildering. In eastern eyes, all life is imbued with spirit — this was an understanding that he had absorbed with his mother's milk. God was everywhere, in every flea, in every mountain. Go to the ends of the universe, and God would be there. Go to the most microscopic level of your bodily cells, and God would be there. To Iqbal, this was as natural as listening to the flute before dawn. Spirit was everywhere, the Vedas said. But what *was* spirit, in scientific terms? And how did it work in evolution? These were the questions that he had sought to understand.

Evolution was yoga, the great Indian sage Sri Aurobindo had said — the longing of the parts to unite with the whole. Yoga meant union, from the Sanskrit word *yuga*, a yoke. Generation after generation of Indians, unaware of geological age, had seen the world as a wheel of suffering which could only be escaped by the conscious realization of the divine. When Aurobindo re-translated the ancient texts with modern eyes, however, he saw a different story. Through evolution, the entire universe was seeking union with the divine, reaching towards ever-greater wholeness and unity.

Iqbal also credited the influence of the French priest and scientist, Pierre Teilhard de Chardin, a Jesuit paleontologist who had spent much of his life in China excavating fossils, unraveling the mysteries of evolution. Like Aurobindo, Teilhard had come to the conclusion that matter and consciousness had evolved together, and that evolution would continue until it reached complete wholeness, when everything would merge with the divine.

The key hypothesis that united Kharoun and Mitchell's work was the proposal that the fundamental building block of all reality was not energy or matter, but consciousness. They described "spirit" as a universal field of consciousness that penetrated and permeated everything. It existed within each of us, but we usually experienced only its trapped individual form. In the Buddhist view, it was as if a tiny dewdrop from the ocean of universal spirit had been dropped into each of us. Humanity's age-old longing for God expressed our deep instinctual desire to reconnect with the whole, for the dewdrop to merge with the ocean. They saw energy, matter and life as evolutionary expressions of consciousness.

Kharoun and Mitchell maintained that under the currently known principles of evolution, there had not been enough time for evolution to have created mind, so there must have been an underlying driving force intent on creating it. This was the anthropic principle. Elizabeth proposed that consciousness pre-existed energy and matter, and that there was a formative force within consciousness which she equated with the Chinese principle of *chi* — hence the *chi-anthropic principle*. It was by communicating through these fields of consciousness that the Kalahari aboriginals and others were able to influence the weather, and perform shamanic deeds. From the chi-anthropic principle to the proposal that syntropy was a fundamental law of nature was just a short step.

The seeds had been sown. The concept that bound it together, which rocketed Iqbal Kharoun and Elizabeth Mitchell onto the front page of *TIME Magazine*, was syntropy. In their words:

> Syntropy is an omnipresent evolutionary tendency which propels all mind, consciousness and matter towards organization, wholeness and unity.

With these eighteen words they had rewritten the modern scientific story. Spirit and syntropy were intimately bound together. When the individual expression of the universal syntropic field was weak, entropy would prevail. Where spirit was strong, syntropy would lead it to seek greater organization and wholeness. It was syntropy that had propelled evolution towards ever more complex and conscious expressions over millions of years. Entropy occurred when syntropy failed, when the spirit in matter weakened and started to die.

With the arrival of syntropy, evolution's entropy problem disappeared. Entropy did not exist at all, Kharoun and Mitchell declared — it was simply the absence of syntropy. It was syntropy which explained evolution's progress towards ever more complex and psychically rich expressions of life, along with humanity's deeply felt drive to achieve peace, freedom, fulfillment, and harmony with nature. The civil rights movement, the women's movement, the peace movement, the environmental movement, the quest to travel into space, the search for renewable energy, the drive for democracy — these were all expressions of syntropy, evolution's fundamental drive for wholeness.

To others, however, these thoughts were blasphemy. To many mainstream scientists they stunk of vitalism, a long-rejected theory that proposed a vital spark within matter. To the Christian fundamentalists, the idea that there was no ultimate separation between God and humans was deeply offensive. To the Islamic fundamentalists, the suggestion that humans could be equals to God was utterly outrageous, and worthy of a *fatwah*.

• • •

After four hours of jogging and hiking, Elizabeth, Iqbal and Amjad reached a beautiful grotto overhung by ferns, surrounded with wildflowers, with a pool of fresh water where they could bathe and drink. Iqbal and Amjad agreed to share lookout duty while Elizabeth took a quick plunge in the pool, and then she proceeded to set up the solar receiver and the satellite transmitter that turned her pocket computer into such a powerful instrument.

"Who shall we send it to?" she asked, when Iqbal returned.

"The world's media. We'd better include PEN International, Amnesty International and the Institute for Consciousness Research, in case the journalists are having a day off. They'll make sure it ends up where it needs to."

It took five minutes to compose the message, and within half an hour their cry for help was appearing on the monitors of journalists, politicians and human rights campaigners all around the world.

"SYNTROPY SCIENTISTS FACE DEATH BY FATWAH. MULLAHS THREATEN TO KILL KHAROUN AND MITCHELL. PRESIDENT ANNOUNCES INDIA TRADE EMBARGO UNLESS FATWAH LIFTED," the headlines and newscasts blared within hours.

In the week that followed, Elizabeth, Iqbal and Amjad took it in turns to keep watch, using their off-duty time to relax in the grotto, bathe in the pool and collect wild fruits and herbs to supplement the dried fruits they had brought in their emergency supplies. The silence and the isolation of the grotto gave them time to work on one of the central missing pieces that their theory still lacked — the need to prove the existence of fields of consciousness in an objective experimental setting. As they talked, exploring the boundaries of such things as telepathy, precognition, absent healing and shamanic magic, Elizabeth knew in her heart that something more was happening, but she received no words of encouragement from Iqbal, and there was never any hint of anything improper. They slept separately, and respected each other's privacy at bathing time. She began to wonder whether it was all in her imagination, brought on by the stress and excitement.

"This will do more to increase public awareness about syntropy theory than we could have achieved in fifty years of lecture tours," Iqbal said one morning when he emerged from meditation. "Maybe they're discussing it in schools around the world, even as we sit here."

"I hope they're sending off protest e-mails as well, if they are!" Elizabeth replied. "It's not as if I have any complaints about being here — it must be one of the most beautiful places on Earth. But I don't sleep well at night, thinking that I might be blasted to hell by a machine gun at any moment."

"Allah will take care of us; Buddha will take care of us; Jesus will take care of us; Krishna will take care of us. What more can we ask?" Iqbal replied — and Elizabeth felt that she wanted to kick him. Or do something else, considerably less violent, that was bottling up inside.

• • •

"I've been thinking," Elizabeth said on their fifth morning at the grotto. "It's about the missing piece, that would change syntropy from a beautiful theory to a proven reality, that would prove that fields of consciousness exist. We've got to find the mechanism that allows syntropy to express itself, that allowed my Kung husband to communicate to a cloud using a rock, or a tree."

"They never let that bother them with entropy. Why should it matter for syntropy?"

"Because it does. So listen. You know those experiments the Russians did in the 1960s, when they separated a mother from her new kittens, and shipped the kittens to the other side of the world? They wired the mother up to an electro-encephalograph, and every time they killed a kitten, the mother's brain-waves jumped."

"Yes. It was cruel, but it did demonstrate a clear connection that something was crossing space instantaneously," Iqbal replied.

"Well — not spontaneously. What if the impulses traveled at 7.48 cycles per second, the speed that light travels around the world? I've been thinking that maybe living beings use the electro-magnetic spectrum at 7.48 cycles per second to communicate with other living beings, and other fields of consciousness — including things like rain clouds, and trees."

"But 7.48 is far below the speed of most normal consciousness."

"Precisely! Oh, Iqbal, sometimes you're so brilliant, you don't see what's right in front of you. If it's true, this might be why it has been so difficult for humans to accept that it is real. It's below the level of conscious awareness that most people have. Animals and plants have it, but not humans — except on the way to sleep, when their brains slow down. So what if we were to set up an experiment using yogis or shamans, people who have mastered a high level of control over their consciousness, and fix them up to a biofeedback machine to help them tune their brains into 7.48 cycles per second — or whatever the exact wavelength is. Then we could ask them to send messages to each other, and test to see if the hypothesis works."

"It might work. But you know what would happen if it did? Some big corporation like SoulTech would come along and claim the patent, and then charge a license fee every time anyone entered the 7.48 zone."

"Then the Indian government would have to gather a bunch of yogis together, to prove that they had the 7.48 expertise long before SoulTech came along," Elizabeth replied with a chuckle.

"And they'd have to train all the judges and the jury in deep meditation techniques, before they could pass any kind of judgment. Come to think of it, they'd have to train the World Trade Organization too — just think of the implications!"

And they burst out laughing.

• • •

That night, while the media and the e-mailers continued their twenty-four-hour struggle to have the *fatwah* lifted, a full moon rose over the mountain, and the grotto became filled with a presence, as if something significant was about to happen.

"I feel as if the whole world is praying for us," Elizabeth said.

"This very true," Amjad chirped in. "Whole world praying for Mr Iqbal and Miss Elizabeth. I feel it here," he added, touching his heart.

"Amjad," Elizabeth replied, "if we get out of this, I'm going to tell the whole world that it is you they should thank. You've been just incredible."

"Miss Elizabeth *will* get out of this. Not *if*," Amjad replied.

"You're amazing, Amjad," Elizabeth said, and went over and kissed him on the forehead. Iqbal watched, with a tender look in his eyes. "I have only known you for these few short weeks, but I love you."

Amjad squirmed, but looked happy.

"Iqbal — we should celebrate," Elizabeth announced. "I don't know what's going to happen tomorrow, whether we shall die or whether we'll be rescued, but I feel that we should celebrate."

"You are quite right, Miss Elizabeth," Iqbal replied, teasingly. "What's stopping us? Let's do it now."

For the next half hour, the two of them carefully cleaned the area around the grotto, while Amjad took a shift on watch. When it was ready, they called Amjad down, and the three of them held hands by the edge of the pool. They could see the moon reflected in the water, and for the next ten minutes they shared words of thanks, appreciation and hope for whatever should follow. Finally, they took it in turns to take water in their hands, to scatter some on the ground to give thanks to nature, and to give it to each other to drink. It was a precious moment that would stay with them for a long time — if they got out of this alive.

Later that night, much later, Iqbal came in from his turn on duty. He saw Elizabeth and Amjad sleeping, but instead of waking Elizabeth to take her turn, he sat down beside her, very quietly. Slowly moving his hands over her body several inches above her sleeping bag, he silently washed her energy field with a blessing of love and appreciation. "I do not know why I am feeling this," he said to himself, "but I think that I love this woman."

Elizabeth stirred, and turning in her bag, saw Iqbal sitting over her. Without thought or hesitation, she reached up and pulled him close.

That moment seemed like an eternity, as all the fronds of accumulated love reached out to seek their goal. Later, they kissed, and unzipping her sleeping bag, she invited him in.

"It's like a glorious song," she whispered to him later, as they held each other close. They had just touched the most incredible place of oneness that either had ever known. "It feels like the song of the whole universe, pouring its love through us. The song of syntropy — and we, its humble recipients."

"I think I like this song," Iqbal whispered in her ear, as he slowly moved his hand through her hair. "I want to hear it forever. Let's leave the last shift, this one night. What will be, will be."

When dawn broke, the five-person search party from the Indian government's conflict resolution team found the three of them fast asleep, in two sleeping bags.

"That's a very peaceful sight," Ashok said to Natasha, as they watched the idyllic scene. "This place feels almost holy."

"Do you know something, Ashok?" Natasha replied. "I think it is."

Notes

The debate around the nature of consciousness and matter and the problems with evolutionary theory are very real. For further information, write to the Institute of Noetic Sciences, 475 Gate Five Road, Suite 300, Sausalito, California, 94965, USA; (415) 331•5650; **www.noetic.org**.

Lyall Watson tells a fascinating story of ethno-climatology in his true-life book about Adrian Boshier's adventures in the South African bush, *Lightening Bird* (Coronet, 1983).

You may treat the 7.48 hypothesis as seriously or as lightly as you wish. There's certainly enough evidence of ancient connectedness and modern telesensory experience to justify continued research into trans-consciousness communication. For an earlier version of this story, written as a straight magazine article, see **www.earthfuture.com/syntropy**.

Donald's Street

"Hey, Jason — can you pass that fantastic red pepper jelly?" Donald called out to his neighbor, who was sitting across the table under the cherry tree. "I can't believe you made it yourself. It's fantastic!"

"Well, it was you who grew the peppers. Take the credit where it's due," Jason replied.

They had been neighbors on Queens Street for ten years, and this was their seventh annual Summer Street Party. Each year, the parties grew better, with more laughter and more creative games and performances. This year, Donald's fourteen-year-old daughter Cristabel and Jason's fifteen-year-old daughter Emma had organized the children on the street into a drama group that was to perform a brief version of *A Midsummer Night's Dream*, presenting all sorts of dubious mischief.

This had all started on January 1st, 2000. On that famous post-Y2K Saturday, after the celebrations of the night before, people all over Victoria had organized Neighbor-to-Neighbor parties to welcome in the new millennium, taking a moment to remember the traditions of good neighborliness before they got lost in the rush. The driving force behind the parties had been a group of people who believed in the need for neighbors to build more resilient communities. They had encouraged neighbors to get together and set up Street Circles as a way to work together as a street or apartment, and take greater control over the streets they lived on. Donald had hosted the New Year's party on Queens Street, and when he had passed around a sheet to see who was interested in forming a Circle, almost everyone had signed up. When they met again three weeks later, they had agreed to create a local Street Directory, to look into traffic reduction on the street, and to organize an annual Summer Street Party.

"Madeleine, was that your cat we heard singing outside our house last night so charmingly?" Donald's wife Kelly asked her neighbor from three doors down. "Maybe she should log onto the cat-personals at cat.com! She might find a handsome mate that way without keeping us awake all night."

"I'm so sorry," Madeleine replied. "My husband says we should get her spayed, but I can't bring myself to do it. Besides, it's so much safer for animals on the street now that the cars have been slowed down."

Five years before, seven of the city's fourteen municipalities had merged to create the Victoria Metropolitan Council, which had organized the formation of neighborhood associations across the whole region, with locally elected councilors. At the same time, the new council had transferred the responsibility for residential street improvements from the Engineering to the Community Development Division. It was a small but very significant change, which announced that from now on, people would have priority over cars on residential streets. Working together in their Street Circle, the residents of Queens Street had looked at a number of ideas for turning their street into a home zone. "This is *your* street," they had been told by the staff at the community development division. "You pay the taxes, and you should have the kind of street you want." They had chosen their design, approved it by a vote of everyone on the street, and raised $5,000 towards the cost of conversion. Everyone had been delighted with the result. In place of the rather boring three-lane road that used to dominate this and so many other suburban streets, they had convinced the community development division to narrow the road down to one lane for a twenty-meter stretch, freeing up the space for the park where they were now enjoying their annual party.

"Excuse me, Donald, but how many varieties of pepper did you say you were growing back there?" his neighbor Elizabeth Lu asked politely.

"Fifteen — you must come over and see them," Donald replied. "I'll trade you for some of those incredible vegetables you've got growing in your yard."

Donald knew that Elizabeth and her husband, Wee-chong, grew a wealth of oriental greens and fruits under the trellis-work which extended from their house, but he had never been invited in, and remained curious as to what they all were. The Lus had listed organic growing as one of their interests in the Street Directory, but good neighborliness did not always extend to an open invitation to enter each other's backyards.

The Whyte family was the complete opposite. They enjoyed chatting with their neighbors over the fence so much that they eventually took down the fence, joining their gardens into one. A neighbor from the back joined in, and soon they were four, with a wonderful space where the children played all day. It was noisy — but everyone knew each other, so they were able to sort it out without the animosity which used to be common in the past, when rowdy parties, noisy cars and barking dogs sometimes set neighbor against neighbor, leading to years of hostile silence.

The main thing that Donald remembered from when he first moved onto Queens Street was nothing specific, simply the absence of relationships. People just didn't talk to each other. It wasn't that they didn't want to — they just didn't know each other, apart from their immediate next-door neighbors. Compared to the 1950s, when he was growing up, people drove to and from their houses instead of walking; they watched television in the evenings instead of playing cards; and they relaxed in their backyards on a summer's evening, instead of sitting on the front porch. After a while, you grew used to the idea that your neighbors came and went, and weren't a part of your life.

Donald was going through a divorce then, having a painful time struggling for the right to see his own daughter. There had been many a night when he'd wished he could walk across to a neighbor's house and talk to someone friendly. That was before the Equal Access Act, which put an end to the years of bitterness when separated parents would use their children as a weapon to try to hurt each other.

When the members of the Queens Street Circle got together to brainstorm ideas for improving their street, they discovered that they wanted more pedestrian paths and back alleys, so that they could get around more easily by bike and on foot without having to follow the roads. They held a meeting with adjacent Street Circles, and took the matter up with their Neighborhood Association. They formed a committee, pored over the maps, and walked all the possible routes for pedestrian paths, or greenways. That led to meetings with the city's other Neighborhood Associations, and before long they had given birth to an entire network of Neighborhood Greenways, complete with a fund to purchase small strips of private backyard where they were needed to create a connection. The whole experience of living in the neighborhood had been transformed by the Greenways.

The traffic calming and the Greenways were part of a larger change in the city's approach to transportation. A comprehensive cycling network had been created, turning some residential back streets into bicycle-priority routes; a light rail transit service was being built to connect Victoria's outlying communities to the city center; and the city's car-share co-operative had been given a grant to help it expand into every neigh-borhood, generating a tenfold increase in the use of its small electric smart cars. The bus service had been improved immensely, with attractive shelters, electronic timetables and a smartcard payment system that gave riders a free bus trip for every ten paid rides. The entire city was beginning to feel different, with less traffic and more smiles.

"Hey, Dad, when can we start the music?" There was soccer, basketball and street hockey happening nearby, but Cristabel was impatient to get started on *A Midsummer Night's Dream*, which they had been practising for weeks. No one knew quite what to expect, but anticipation was running high.

"In a while, dear. Just give us old farts a chance to relax before we start changing the world. And remember — you promised to let me do my Madonna impersonation!"

Changing the world was an apt description for some of the things that the Queens Street Circle had been up to. Two years before, in 2004, the solar revolution had kicked in, with competitively priced solar shingles becoming available through the Internet. Working through their Street Circle, ten households had negotiated a group discount. With the roofs installed, they were obtaining half of their annual electricity needs from the new shingles. On a hot summer's day like today, they were selling the surplus back to the grid through an arrangement called "net-metering," which helped them pay for the cost of installation.

Then last year, following the death of a forty-five-year-old neighbor from cancer of the liver, they had decided that their front yards should become a pesticide-free zone, to reduce the risk of dogs and children tracking toxic chemicals back into their homes, where they became embedded in carpets and too often, found their way into the mouths of babies. This spring, two teenagers had organized a neighborhood contest to see which street could boast the greatest number of non-toxic households, which Queens Street had won. They had also initiated a backyard wildlife program, and started a tradition of inviting new residents on the street to a "Meet the Neighbors" party. They were small changes, but they made a difference.

Then there was the Street History Project. The young people had done all the legwork, interviewing the oldest residents and digging into the archives to find out about the earlier owners and the history of particular houses, tracking the history of Queens Street right back to when it had been a forest. The youngsters had been given a helping hand by the new Community History Project, and they had published their research on the Internet, with an abbreviated version in the front of the Queens Street Directory. The project had created lots of interest, and given the street a stronger sense of its own identity.

"DAD! You promised!" Cristabel's voice rang out. Oh, the impatience of youth.

"OK, everyone. We'd better get on with it," Donald said to his neighbors as they relaxed in the shade on this wonderful sunny Sunday evening. "Roll out the troops!"

"YES!" Cristabel responded, and rushed to gather up her friends from the soccer tournament. The magic was about to begin.

earthfuture

Notes

At the time of writing (August 1999), the January 1ˢᵗ 2000 Neighbor-to-Neighbor parties are being planned. The initiative to organize Street Circles is organized by the United Way through the Street Volunteers program (**www.greenpages.victoria. bc.ca/streetvolunteers**). In Holland, many local streets have been turned into home zones, where children, pets and neighborly activities take priority over cars. Britain is now following their example.

The Victoria Car-Share Co-operative was founded in 1997 (**www.com/~carshare**); the members of the Greater Victoria Cycling Coalition (**www.gvcc.bc.ca**) have been responsible for most of the cycling improvements in the city. Whenever creative changes happen in our communities, you'll usually find an organized non-profit society behind them.

Solar shingles are being installed on houses in Japan, Germany, Britain and Holland. The secret lies with net-metering, an arrangement whereby the local power utility pays the homeowner a decent price for surplus solar or wind-generated power which is fed back into the grid. An Internet search on "solar shingles" will lead you to the relevant contacts.

A Bike! A Bike!

A bike! A bike! My Island for a bike!

Oh, that the sweetest lanes and mountaintops
Should not with foul assault be shaven,
Worthlessly to fall from glorious gold
Into the lost debris of myths that once were golden.

For doth this Island that we love so much
Touch not the very heavens with its grace?
Do not the eagles e'en look down with joy
As in its air they spire their ancient dance?

What fools be we if, in our late arriving,
We do destroy the place of our arrival,
Burying deep its heart, its soul
In the rubble of our building.

Such is the brilliance of excess,
The wisdom that can only see
Delight in a supermarket trolley,
Not a tree.

Bring then a bike, a train, a humble bus
That we should change this climate in our souls
Before we burn the planet on our coals.
This appetite will be the death of us.

earthfuture

Bring me a bike! A tram! A rollerblade!
Than pave this heaven someone made.
Take hence this thing that's hagged its might
Into the mare of all our nights.

In place of haste and rush and greed
Let's place sweet limits on our speed,
And in constraint, let's say a prayer
For bikes — God bless them, everywhere.

The Natural Step

Portland, Oregon
October 2007

It was a brisk fall morning when Jack Wilkinson followed a crowd of fifty of his customers down the shady paths of Mount Hood National Forest, an hour outside Portland. The towering red cedars and western hemlocks gave the forest a cathedral-like atmosphere, which had the visitors enthralled. Pausing underneath a giant Douglas fir, the forester explained how he selected his trees for felling, taking care to leave a balance of trees of all ages, preserving the strongest to produce seeds for the next generation.

Jack had arranged the day-trip to show his customers where their furniture came from, and had been astonished by the response. "We'll get maybe five or ten to sign up," he had told his son Mark, who had suggested the outing. When the entire bus filled up, and the customers started chatting to each other, he had to admit that he had under-estimated their enthusiasm for the changes that he and Mark had introduced to the company.

Jack had been working for Wilkinson's Furniture, his father's small twenty-person furniture-making business in Portland, ever since he left college with a business degree in 1975. Instead of letting him manage the company, however, his father had apprenticed him to a trained craftsman, making him start at the bottom. He had spent ten years learning the craft before his father allowed him to join him at the top.

He enjoyed producing the bookshelves and William Morris chairs that Wilkinson's Furniture was known for, but he had always felt there was something missing in his life, in spite of his supposedly happy marriage and his two successful children. It was like that wistful song — "Is that all there is?" He was a tall, quiet man, with a thin face and a shy manner. For all of his adult life, he had been plagued with voices inside his head that

41

fussed at him, like an irritating burr caught inside his sock. *"Are you sure you're doing the right thing? You didn't do that very well. You're such a disappointment. When are you going to get on with your life?"*

For the last few months, however, the voices had been silent. He could enjoy the October sun as it shone through the trees without telling himself that he should be working. It felt strangely wonderful. Was this a temporary trick that his life was playing on him, he asked himself, or was it going to be permanent?

His son Mark had come straight into the business after leaving school. He seemed to have his grandfather's talent for making beautiful furniture. It must have skipped a generation, Jack thought. He was competent at his craft, but he had never shown any kind of brilliance. He was a dull, boring man — that was his judgment of himself.

His daughter Nancy had been the wild one, leaping from rock-climbing and mountain-biking to twenty-four-hour charity relays, jumping at new challenges whenever they arose. When Nancy opened her eyes to the destruction that was happening to the natural world and threw herself into environmental causes, chaining herself to bulldozers and hoisting herself into the canopies of old-growth trees, her mother, Julia, was shocked at their daughter's unruly ways, but Jack silently delighted in the way she had cast off any notion of "career" to follow the dictates of her conscience. If things had been different, perhaps he could have been as free, as independent. He knew that there was a hole in the ozone layer, and that the salmon were in crisis, but the bottom line was that he had a business to manage, and besides, these things weren't his responsibility.

Then Nancy had been killed in a terrible car crash. On Sunday night, she was bouncing around on the sofa with her brother Mark, filling their home with joy. By Monday lunchtime, she was dead. Jack was astonished to see a thousand people show up at her funeral, crying so openly, while he held back his tears. Only later, when no one could see him, would he allow himself to weep.

Nancy had always been after him to change the way Wilkinson's Furniture did its business. She wanted him to start using wood from forests that were eco-certified and managed sustainably. She wanted him to stop using toxic glues and finishes. She wanted him to use a bicycle delivery service for the smaller orders, instead of a truck. *Oh Dad*, she would say, *I wish you would listen to me*.

Jack listened, but he never acted on her requests. It wasn't an easy business, selling furniture. There was so much competition from Thailand and Indonesia, where the workers earned a tenth of the wages. With the slightest slip, the whole business could disappear, along with all of their jobs. *Stick with what we do best*, his father had drilled into him. *Don't take any unnecessary risks. Our business must be like our furniture — solid and reliable.*

It was his son Mark who had unintentionally started the sequence of events that led to his being here in the forest on a Saturday morning, instead of playing golf with his friends from the Lions Club. Mark had designed an elegant but simple lamp holder, which had attracted the attention of IKEA, the Swedish furniture giant. IKEA had test-marketed the holder in its Portland and Seattle stores, and then invited Jack to supply them with 40,000 a year. When Jack and Mark met with IKEA, however, they learned that there was one clause in the contract that was non-negotiable.

IKEA had an environmental policy that was printed inside a little booklet which they gave to all their employees: *At IKEA, we shall always strive to minimize any possible damaging effects to the environment which may result as a consequence of our activities*. That was Jack's first introduction to The Natural Step, a Swedish system of environmental design which had been created eighteen years earlier to help businesses, governments and communities re-organize themselves along ecological lines, instead of contributing to the deterioration of the natural world.

Joel was IKEA's purchasing manager in Portland. "The planet Earth is like a spacecraft," he had told Jack and Mark as they sat in his tenth-floor office suite at their first meeting. "It is all alone in this huge dark cosmos. On this Earth, we have been given a gift called nature, and we have to look after her, or we will all be the losers." He took a jug and poured a glass of water. "Nature contains water, for instance," he said, "but there will never be more than there is today. These molecules of water may be the same molecules which were drunk by the dinosaurs, or by Julius Caesar. In due course, they may be drunk by our great, great grandchildren. Matter and energy can never be created nor destroyed — but they can easily disperse, creating pollution and waste, unless we take care not to disperse them." These were the First and Second Laws of Thermodynamics, which Jack had learned at school. They were also the first two principles of The Natural Step.

"Whenever we release carbon from fossil fuels into the atmosphere," Joel continued, "it stays there, adding to the greenhouse effect. Whenever we destroy topsoil through careless logging, we lose it forever — it takes nature thousands of years to create new topsoil. In IKEA, we try to take care of our employees and our customers. We try to create a quality product of which everyone can be proud. And we try to take care of the planet, since it is the only one we have."

It all seemed so natural. When Nancy had tried to tell Jack the same thing, it had sounded like a dream — nice, but unrealistic. Coming from IKEA, it seemed to make sense.

Jack and Mark had their meeting with Joel the week before Christmas in 2004. After he left the IKEA office, Jack did some Christmas shopping and then went home to pour himself a beer and watch the video Joel had given them. Julia was working late at the law firm. It was a year since Nancy had died, and though Jack did not know it, it would be their last Christmas together as a family. The following spring, Julia would walk out on Jack, leaving him for an older man with a large yacht and a yen to sail around the world. "You're too boring for me," she said, as she packed her cases. "I need to find some adventure in my life."

The video started with the familiar image of planet Earth floating gently in space. Then to the heavenly harmonies of English cathedral choirboys, it showed the daily rhythm by which businesses in the Portland area mined, logged, shipped, manufactured, consumed and discarded raw materials. The contrast between the music and the video was quite disturbing. Every day, Portland businesses and consumers were causing the erosion of the Earth's ecological integrity, both locally and globally. The chemicals that were released in the manufacture of plywood were left to drift in the air, to be absorbed by children and adults, birds and animals. The oil that was spilled on the way to the gas pumps was lost into the oceans, killing the sea-birds. Forests were being cut down to feed the hunger for wood; mangrove swamps were being bulldozed to feed the hunger for shrimps. All over the city, businesses were allowing their chemical wastes to escape into the drains and, via the Columbia river, into the ocean. Portland did a great job of recycling, but the volume of waste that was still being dumped or which was escaping into the air or water was appalling.

Then the video's focus shifted, and people from businesses around the world spoke about the changes they were making. The CEO of the Swedish hotel chain, Scandic, spoke about the 2,000 different environmental initiatives they had brought in, down to such tiny things as changing the way they dispensed their soap. A director of the Portland Catalogue clothing company explained how they had saved $10,000 in a single year by replacing the throw-away paper cups at their vending machine with a "bring-your-own-mug" policy. The president of the international shoe company, Nike, told how they had redesigned their famous running shoes to eliminate the non-organic solvent adhesives, and make the entire shoe recyclable.

The video showed how, since the 1990s, there had been a change in the Oregon air, and an exciting new vitality. The state was moving beyond its forestry and fishing past, re-inventing itself as a land of high technology and environmental opportunities. Ordinary people had realized that there could be life after logging, and opposition to environmental reforms had weakened. Capitalizing on the new sympathy, in 2002 the Oregon State Legislature had replaced the local sales tax with an adjustable tax based on ecological impact. Using custom-made software called ECO-it, every product sold in Oregon was graded according to its eco-impact. The grade was incorporated into the product's bar-code, where it could be read by a scanner and the product taxed accordingly. The scheme was controversial, but the government stuck to its guns. Why tax all products equally, the governor argued, when some did more damage to the environment than others? Under the new system, products with a higher ecological impact would incur higher taxation, which would encourage their producers to clean up their act.

In wrapping up, the video showed how the Portland office of The Natural Step had played a significant role in the changes. From small beginnings in the 1990s, it was now approaching the Portland Metropolitan Chamber of Commerce, with a view to involving its 35,000 members. "We invite every business in Portland to join us," the narrator said, "so that our whole economy can begin to operate according to nature's principles."

"One step at a time," the video concluded. Jack was hooked. He called IKEA's office to say yes, he would accept their conditions, and the next morning he gathered his workers together and showed them the video. That was three years ago.

When Jack and Mark returned to Wilkinson's Furniture after IKEA's two-day Natural Step training session, they had a long list of "small steps" which would enable their business to harmonize with nature's principles. It would take time, but so did everything. The glues and finishes would have to be replaced; the whole building would need an energy retrofit; the older, less-efficient equipment would have to be replaced; their methods of packing and shipping would have to be upgraded. The biggest change, however, which had to happen immediately if they wanted to secure the IKEA order, was that their timber would have to come from an eco-certified, sustainably managed forest.

That was how Jack found out about Collins Pine, a forest products company operating out of Portland, which was another member of The Natural Step. Collins managed 300,000 acres of forest along eco-certified lines, and when Jack went to visit the managers, they were more than happy to supply him with the timber Wilkinson's needed. "But first," they said, "you must come and tour our forest, to understand how it differs from a regular forest."

Jack had been dealing with timber all his life, but this was the first time he had ever toured a sustainably managed forest, or learned about ecosystem management. His guide was Sophie, who had been a practising ecoforester for five years.

"We never cut more than nature grows," she explained, as she showed Jack around their Almanor forest in the Sierra Nevada. "We have been logging these 94,000 acres since 1943. We have extracted almost two billion board-feet of timber, and yet the forest has a higher inventory of standing timber today than when we started, and it still has its old-growth characteristics." Jack was impressed by how open the forest was, and how large the trees were. "If we had clearcut the way the other companies did," Sophie went on, "we would have destroyed the soil and habitat, and we would be harvesting much less timber today, of lower quality. The way to get the value out of this kind of forest while protecting the ecosystem is to maximize the age of the trees at around 150 years, not cut them down when they are immature juveniles."

That night, as Jack slept in an ecotourist cabin in the forest, he had a powerful dream. He was walking in the forest, and he saw his daughter Nancy coming towards him, carrying a bundle of ferns and wildflowers. She was smiling, and the forest was full of birds and wildflowers. Coming close, she placed the bundle in his hands, and said "Here — this is yours now," and then disappeared.

That was two years ago. Now, Jack was in another forest with another tour guide, and with the loyal customers who had supported him as he led Wilkinson's Furniture on its journey of transformation. The word had spread about the changes they were making, the media had featured them as an Oregon success story, and the orders had begun to increase. Now, he was employing an additional forty people to meet the demand.

The forester had paused and was pointing up to a towering fir tree, over 200 years old. "This is one of our seed trees," he explained. "I call her Old Molly. She's like a grandmother, she has so many children. We don't plant trees any more — we simply protect the ones with the best features, and let them do it for us."

"But isn't that a lot slower than planting new trees in an organized manner?" someone asked.

"Not at all," the forester replied. "And furthermore, when you leave the trees to regenerate naturally, they grow a much tighter timber, which makes better furniture. You should see some of the rubbish that's growing in the commercial plantations, where they still do it the old way. The trees are all skinny and packed together, their cells fat and blousy, because they've been absorbing so much light. The timber warps when it dries out. Makes lousy furniture. That right, Jack?"

Jack nodded. He had witnessed the gradual deterioration of the timber they used in the shop, but he had never understood why. "I'll tell you a secret, Matty," Jack replied in a voice that everyone could hear, "as long as you promise not to tell anyone else." There was a chuckle, as his customers appreciated his dry sense of humor. Had he always had this humor Jack wondered, or was it just beginning to come out now that he was a single man? "The truth is, I never understood why the timber was getting worse. I just assumed it was one of those things that was destined to go downhill, like television, and the way the kids like to dress. I've learned a lot since then."

He didn't know it, but his customers were slowly growing to love him for his honesty and lack of pretense.

I wonder, he thought to himself as he watched his customers gather round a dead fir tree that was being preserved as a wildlife tree, to sustain the woodpeckers which kept the insects under control. *Is this perhaps the reason why my voices have disappeared, why I have this feeling of contentment? Could it be, at the age of fifty-six, that I have finally found my own path?*

He smiled to himself, and realized that for the first time, he was enjoying the feeling of his own feet being planted solidly on the forest floor. There was a flapping of wings in the trees, and an eagle's feather landed softly at his feet.

Notes

My thanks to Brian Nattrass, Mary Altomare, Bill Robson and Kate Wells for their help with this story. The Natural Step is a Swedish initiative which is winning increasing praise around the world for its capacity to help companies and other organizations harmonize their activities with nature, re-organizing themselves along ecological lines. See *The Natural Step for Business: Wealth, Ecology and the Evolutionary Corporation*, by Brian Nattrass and Mary Altomare (New Society Publishers, 1999), or visit **www.NaturalStep.org**.

- In Canada: Brian Nattrass, (604) 886•0937, tns@aol.com.
- In Portland: Kate Wells, (503) 241•1140, ktwells@aol.com.
- In San Francisco: Catherine Gray, (415) 561•3344, tns@naturalstep.org
- In Britain: David Cook, (01242) 262744, davidcook@tnsuk.demon.co.uk

The information about IKEA (**www.ikea.com**), Collins Pine (**www.collins wood.com**) and other companies is true. The Dutch software ECO-it has been developed by PRi Consultants, and can aid in the design of environmentally responsible products and packaging, enabling a product's environmental impact to be expressed in one figure. A demo can be downloaded from **www.pre.nl**. It has not yet been used for the purposes of eco-taxation.

Kamchatka's Reprieve

From Tanya Dobretsova,
Oktyabr'skiy, Kamchatka, in Russia's far east
June 21st, 2008

My dearest Igor,

Are you enjoying your life in Seattle? We are camped by the ocean on the Sea of Okhotsk, watching the sun set while we enjoy a supper of freshly caught char baked on larch wood, served on a bed of greens which our guide has been gathering all day. What bliss!

This place is stupendous. Growing up in Moscow, I knew Russia was big, but I always thought the far east meant Vladivostok — next stop Japan, then San Francisco. This place is something completely else. In the last four weeks I have seen so many brown bears, sea eagles, ospreys, foxes and other wildlife that I have used up all my film, and it'll be two weeks before I can buy any more. The birdlife here is unbelievable — there are such huge numbers of everything. And not just ducks and geese, but sea lions, seals, bowhead whales and sea otters. They say there are grey whales out there somewhere. Last night I saw a sea hawk plunge out of nowhere onto a group of ducks, and make off with her supper.

We bumped into a group of Americans last week. We were swimming in the nude together at some hot springs, near one of Kamchatka's many geysers, and I discovered they were with Intercrop, the logging company that's been causing so many concerns. The last I'd heard, they were trying to negotiate with the regional government to release an additional hundred thousand hectares for so-called responsible logging — that means hiding the clearcuts where no one can see them, the way they used to do in Canada. It's one aspect of this trip that I've found constantly disturbing — the presence of international logging companies, slowly working their way down the coast. They want to log paradise, to put up a timber lot.

But Igor! They told us there had been a major collapse in the global pulp market, for reasons they didn't explain, and that their parent company had told them to put most of their logging on hold. They also said that because of the growing demand for timber that had been grown and harvested in an ecologically certified manner, Intercrop was going to have to give up the huge clearcuts they've been doing in recent years, and go back to the way forestry used to be in Russia before the free market changes, with hundred-meter water protection zones for the smallest streams, and no logging on steep slopes or unstable soils.

They didn't say why the pulp market was collapsing; something about electronic stuff taking over, and some jokes about hemp. I think they were more interested in us than the global pulp market. You know what men are like, when they spend too long together out in the forests.

How much longer are you going to be stuck in the city? You'd love it out here. I don't know when you'll get these scribblings. I'll try to find a computer the next time we're near a settlement, so that I can scan this over to you.

Until then, with my love,
Your Tanya

• • •

From Igor Bodrov
Seattle, Washington
June 30th

Dear Tanya,

How good to read your scribblings! I passed your letter around the office — you've become quite a local celebrity here. Everyone is asking, "When's her next letter coming?" They all expect you to show up one day, to live with me.

My life is unbelievably boring over here. Maybe I'm just not cut out for the city life. It has been so cold! We're past midsummer's day, and people say they still can't plant their tomatoes outside. The office is just bursting with tomatoes in pots, yellowing at the tips, waiting to go out. On top of that, it has been the wettest summer ever. "Welcome to Seattle," they say, but they're not enjoying it either. It's a long way from where you are.

Your logger friends are quite right about the pulp industry. The traditional market for pulp is finished, except for some specialty markets like greetings cards. Global Media filed for bankruptcy last month, bringing down some 850 daily newspapers, including the *New York Times* and the *Sun*, in England, in spite of their attempts to publish electronic versions. Nobody I know reads printed newspapers anymore. You wait till you get back to Moscow — I'm sure it'll be the same there. It's happening so quickly! The latest electronic tablets are so pleasant to read and so light to carry around, and the stories they carry are so much higher quality. They're rapidly replacing newspapers and magazines all over America. It's the same with books, which are being pushed aside by the new electronic bookframes, or ebook.

They were right about hemp, too, Tanya. There are a lot of farmers growing it as a serious agricultural crop. They use it to make tree-free paper, hemp clothing, oil and all sorts of things. It's not just the hemp, either. There's also paper being made from recycled paper and agricultural wastes, primarily rice straw, which was always a headache for the rice growers. They weren't allowed to burn it; it cost them too much to truck away for composting; and if they ploughed it in, it caused stem rot. The quantities were unbelievable, so when a Canadian engineer developed a process for turning it into paper, a bunch of rice farmers in California helped him finance a string of community-based pulp mills, and they were in business. They're using it to build straw-bale houses, too — I've been in one. It has twice the insulation of a traditional wooden building, and must be lovely to live in. It's all round and cosy at the corners. They said it was easy to construct, and there's enough straw in America to meet the residential building needs of the entire country. It's only a matter of time before someone brings the idea to Russia. Think of those millions of wheat fields east of Moscow, and all that straw which could be used for building. If we don't need trees to make paper any more, and we don't need so much timber to build our houses, why do we need to log in a place like Kamchatka at all?

I'd better get back to work. They've got me designing an interface for a new consumer product that will allow parents to do their own genetic code analysis on their children, with a built-in encryption system to prevent anyone from trying to steal a DNA sample if the children happen to have a rare gene. I must admit, I find the whole thing rather disturbing.

With love,
Igor

P.S. Did you tell your mother about our separation?

• • •

Klyuchi
July 25ᵗʰ

Dear Igor,

It was so good to hear from you. What separation? Do you mean about you being in Seattle and me here? Yes, of course I told her.

You won't believe where we've been these last two weeks. After spending two weeks camped around Oktyabr'skiy, getting bitten to pieces by the bugs, we headed north into the mountains, then down into the Kamchatka Valley. It is so lush, green and moist, it almost makes you want to eat it. Why aren't you here to enjoy it with me, I ask myself?

There has been no sign of any active logging in the valley — but we had an ugly encounter with a bunch of hunters a week ago. They said they were from Canada on an ecotourism experience, but when Nikolai lifted the canvas on their all-terrain vehicle it had the bodies of not one but five brown bears in it. I was sick. It was quite funny, looking back on it. I puked up all over this hunter's pants and he got really mad, rushing around like he'd got rabies. Then Nikolai showed them his wildlife exploration permit from the Kamchatka Regional Committee for Nature Protection, hoping to calm things down, but this got their guide rattled. He thought Nikolai was some kind of government official. They took off at top speed, bears and all, shouting back at us, "Bloody government! Bloody regulations!" It's hopeless, Igor — the Kamchatka peninsula is so large, and it's impossible to track what the hunters are doing once they're here. Luckily we managed to get a digital video of them, which I'm sending with this e-mail. Can you forward it to the World Bear Protection Society? They've got a website where they show footage of the bear hunters in action, mostly in Russia and Northern China. They use the data to embarrass the hunters and pressure the Russian and Chinese governments into signing the Global Treaty on Endangered Species. They also send the video-clips to the hunting outfits, to say, "We know what you're doing."

For the past week we've been going to bed and waking up to the sight of this stunning snow-capped volcano, Klyuchevskaya Sopka. Words fail me — I can't begin to describe how beautiful everything is around here. I wish you were here with me, so that we could wake up together, and share this astonishment. Yesterday we spent the morning watching a pair of snow rams wandering on the side of the mountain. It's no wonder they made it a World Heritage Site. If we can be sure the logging is going to stop, and if we can stop the hunting, this whole peninsula might return to the peaceful glory it must have enjoyed for ever, until modern "progress" found it. We've also been told that the companies have put their oil exploration plans for the sea of Okhotsk on hold — they say that by the time any oil comes on line, the market will have weakened to the extent that it will no longer be commercially viable. Long live solar energy!

Out here, surrounded by the mountains, the birch trees, and the eagles, your work with genetic software sounds like something from another planet. It sounds scary. I'm intrigued by the electronic tablet you mentioned, though. What is it, exactly? You know how backward we are in Moscow. What are these electronic books? Does it mean I'll have to read my Tolstoy and Pushkin on some kind of computer screen? I can't think of anything worse.

I hope your weather has warmed up, and that your tomatoes are happy by now. Are you keeping warm yourself? One of the scientists in our team told me that the salmon had stopped returning to Washington and Oregon because the ocean was too warm, and they were dying before they could reach the rivers. Is this true? There are still salmon in the rivers here, but the local fishing people are very troubled by the arrival of some commercial fish farms. They know what happened in Scotland, Norway and British Columbia, where the diseases from the fish farms killed enormous numbers of wild salmon, and they are afraid it will happen here.

We're heading off to the Komandorskiye Islands tomorrow, to see how the sea otters, blue foxes and red foxes are doing. They had the islands to themselves until Captain Vitus Bering was shipwrecked there in 1741 with a crew of Russians. They were forced to spend the winter there, and the crew started killing the otters and the foxes for their furs, setting off one of the greatest slaughters in marine history. They're finally beginning to recover, which is good news. It's pretty wild out there, so it'll be a couple of weeks before you hear from me again. And darling Igor, please don't forget that while I may be separate from you in distance, my heart is entwined with yours.

With my love, as ever,
Tanya

• • •

Seattle
August 3rd

Dear Tanya,

I thought we had agreed that we would separate while I was in Seattle. Please don't make life difficult for me. I still love you, and I will always be your friend, but I need my freedom. I want to celebrate both love *and* freedom. Can you not, too?

Your enthusiasm for the beauty of Klyuchevskaya Sopka inspired me to take off with a friend for a weekend's camping on Mount Rainier, just south of Seattle. I love this place. It is like heaven on earth once you get out of the city. Helen is someone I met at a meeting in the office last week, who has known the mountain since she was a child, and she showed me some of the secret places and back trails where there are hardly any hikers. So I, too, have been camping with the mountain beside me. I thought about you as I gazed at the Pacific Ocean out to the west, watching the sun set. On the far side of that water, I thought, there's Tanya, talking to the sea otters. You'd like Helen. She has the same love of the wild that you do.

You asked about the tablets. Technically, they're ultra-thin, ultra-light screens you can carry around with you and read in comfort wherever you like. That's part of their charm, that they've broken the SAAD barrier (that's nerdish for Stuck At A Desk). They sell for under $100, and are not really computers at all — it's just a screen, which you can read wherever you want. That's the whole joy of it. You plug it into a modem or cable attachment, download the features from whichever news service you have subscribed to, and walk away with it. Who needs a printed newspaper, when you can have something as simple as this? If you want more detail on a particular story, you can connect to a modem and dig into the hyperpages on the Internet, where there are deeper layers of information. It's an advertiser's dream, of course. If you are interested in something they're advertising, you just hook up, click on the box and order whatever it is right then and there, as you do on the Internet.

But that's only half of it. You remember when we were students in Moscow, how we used the Internet to obtain most of our quality information? We used to be on all sorts of lists, receiving newsletters and digests. The tablet news services work the same way, but in a much more organized manner. When you sign on to one of the services, they ask you what your interests are, and at which level you want to receive the information, and they tailor the news to meet your needs. You can still explore other areas of the news for the fun of exploring, but if you don't want the hockey, you don't get the hockey. It's light years ahead of the old-fashioned printed media, which needed forests to be cut down, their topsoils ruined and their wildlife scattered to the winds to bring us pages and pages of paper, most of which we never read.

I'm not a religious kind of guy, as you know, but it feels as if God looked down on the forests, felt compassion for the centuries of destruction they suffered at the hands of humanity, and decided to give them one everlasting gift: the electronic tablet.

It's the same with books. The new ebooks are selling like hotcakes in Seattle's bookshops and supermarkets. There's a huge range of covers, from old-fashioned leather bindings with gilded decorations to ultra-modern designs using the latest DNA-art. I chose one with a blank design, which displays the cover of whatever book I'm reading. Inside, it is like a book, but with a screen on either side. You plug it into one of the new electronic bookshops, choose from among the zillion or so titles that are available, pay for it on-line and download it into your bookframe. Once it's there, you can take it away to read in bed, in a hammock, or even in the bath — just like a normal book, but better. You can adjust the print size and the font; you can even order it in a different language, if you want to. Are you happy yet?

I bought my first electronic book last week — the prize-winning novel by the Polish poet Wanda Wadolna, *Maria's Farm*. Because of the new electronic format, she is able to include photographs and film footage of the locations, and the houses where the characters live. In one episode, where the characters are listening to a Rachmaninoff piano concerto while talking together at night, you can plug the book in and listen to the same concerto while you read. In the hyperpages she has included several additional subplots, along with extra details about the characters, and their backgrounds. For the major love scenes, she offers you a choice of descriptions according to your taste — mild, hot or superhot, just like a curry. The superhot version is very steamy and explicit, but equally well written. These new bookframes are going to turn the traditional world of novel-writing completely upside-down.

For non-fiction books, you can highlight and store sections of the text, search the text electronically, and then dig into the book's hyperpages via the Internet to connect to a reference, or the author's home page — just like the electronic tablets. It's beginning to be considered cheap for a book to have no additional layers. In *Maria's Farm*, there's a section where she describes this idyllic bicycle tour through the old city of Lublin and the surrounding countryside, with a mark indicating a hyperpage connection. So I plugged in, clicked on the mark, and there were the details of a cycling expedition through the region, including a night in the very house where the heroine spends a passionate night of love at the climax of the book. This is going to be great for the authors, who will be able to benefit from all the commercial spin-offs.

So don't worry, Tanya. You'll still be able to have your beloved Pushkin:

And Memory before my wakeful eyes
With noiseless hand unwinds her lengthy scroll.

While I'll have my Anna Akhmatova:

Low in the sky there shines a star
Between two trunks of trees.
So calmly promising to me
That what I dream, shall be.

And through the hyperpages, we'll be able to visit our poets' homelands, gazing on their landscapes and immersing ourselves in their worlds. You'll be able to open the door to a Pushkin Café and share your thoughts with other Pushkin lovers. It's a whole new world of literature, Tanya. Here in Seattle, the bookshops are scrambling to reinvent themselves, before they are driven out of business.

For so many years, we accepted that our beloved forests had to be destroyed in order to produce the books we love. Oh Tolstoy, how many trees must have fallen because you loved Natasha and Pierre so much, you gave them 700 pages?

Living here in Seattle, I have been able to see first-hand how much paper the modern world has been using — all cut from the forest. I've dug out some data, because it's so shocking. Writing paper, newspaper, cardboard, flyers, boxes, magazines, tissue paper — the volume was amazing. The average American consumed 350 kilograms of paper and cardboard a year — that's a tonne and a half for a family of four. Five percent was used for packaging; forty-three percent for holding ink in books, newspapers, and magazines; and seven percent for tissues, toilet paper, and paper towels. They say the streets of London were drowning in horse manure before the motor car came along. Well, North America was drowning in paper from the world's forests, thousands of years old, being turned into the dross of junk flyers, telephone books and newspapers.

Thanks to the tablet, the bookframe, and similar changes in the world of building materials, those rich and glory-filled forests of Kamchatka will no longer have to be cut down to satisfy the world's hunger for pulp or cheap timber. There is even a mini-revolution happening in the world of cardboard packaging, thanks to the development of ultra-durable, see-through plastic boxes which can be assembled and disassembled up to a thousand times before they have to be recycled. We just have to tighten the ecological clauses on timber sales in the World Ecological Trade Treaty that is due to be negotiated in Paris next year, and Kamchatka's forests will be safe forever.

Well, I'd better finish before my supervisor realizes I'm not working. Did you know that scientists in Texas are taking the genes from a spider and inserting them into a horse to create an eight-legged horse which will be able to run twice as fast? Just kidding.

Your friend,
Igor

P.S. Helen says hello. I've told her about you and me, and she thinks that's great. She's very open-minded about things like this. I wonder if all American women are the same?

- For Tanya's reply A, see http://www.earthfuture.com/Kamchatka/A
- For Tanya's reply B, see http://www.earthfuture.com/Kamchatka/B
- For Tanya's reply C, see http://www.earthfuture.com/Kamchatka/C
- For Tanya's reply D, see http://www.earthfuture.com/Kamchatka/D

Notes

The Kamchatka peninsula is one of the world's amazing places, but for proof that bear-hunting tourism is going on, see **www.ameri-cana.com/rbrbear.htm**. It will cost you $6,400 for a week's hunting, plus $2,500 for a trophy kill. The World Bear Protection Society is imaginary, but Bear Watch (PO Box 405, Ganges, Salt Spring, British Columbia, V8K 2W1, Canada) does equivalent work.

The information about Captain Vitus Bering and his sailors' slaughter of the sea otters on the Komandorskiye Islands is true. See *The Nature of Sea Otters: A Story of Survival,* by Stefani Paine and Jeff Foott (Greystone Books).

Russia's forests used to be far more protected before the arrival of the free market. For details, see **www.greenpeace.org/~forests/russia/wheritkamchatka.html**. The Forest Stewardship Council is leading the revolution in eco-certified timber, which is going to transform forestry the way that organic farming is transforming agriculture. (Forest Stewardship Council, PO Box 10, Waterbury, Vermont, 05676, USA; (802) 244•6257; info@fscus.org; **http://fscus.org**). The World Ecological Trade Treaty does not yet exist.

After writing this story, I learned about the Rocket ebook, a screen the size of a paperback that can hold 4,000 pages of words and images, and sells for $495 — see www.ebookempire.com/. Now I just have to arrange to get this published as an ebook!

For information on tree-free paper — if you do a search on "tree-free paper" you'll be astonished how much is out there, from hemp to bamboo paper. For straw-bale buildings, see *The Straw Bale House* (Chelsea Green, 1994) and *Straw Bale Building* (New Society Publishers, 2000).

Pushkin's lines come from *Remembrance*, translated by Maurice Baring. Anna Akhmatova's lines are from *Love Poems*, translated by Natalie Duddington, both from the *Penguin Book of Modern Verse Translation* (Penguin Books, 1966).

Farewell to Toxics

Gold River, British Columbia
March 2009

It was another wet morning in Gold River, but when Sophie read the article on her morning tablet, her spirits soared higher than the bald eagles that inhabited the forest behind her cottage.

"Following Monday's statement by Mongrando that the company would be pulling fifteen of its leading pesticides, herbicides and other products containing proven toxic ingredients off the market, and phasing out another ninety, Dowager Chemicals, AgroNovalis and Hosch International yesterday announced that they would no longer manufacture the toxic products. Laura Keelover, a spokeswoman for Dowager, said that their entire North American inventory would be reviewed over the next six months. The shares of all four companies jumped sharply as the markets responded, sensing that the clouds which had been hanging over the chemical giants' future had been removed."

Sophie wanted to rush out and tell someone, but the quiet cottage where they lived on the side of a mountain on the far west coast of Vancouver Island, near the tiny village of Gold River, had no immediate neighbors. Max was away at his canoe workshop in town; Sylvan, their five-year-old son, was at school; and Esperanza, their one-year-old daughter, was asleep. Sophie spoke to her cat, Molly.

"No more hidden pesticides in your dried food — do you hear that, Molly? No more worrying about what you're going to bring home on your paws off people's lawns when you wander into town. Whoopee!" She picked Molly up and waltzed her around their living room, cradled in her arms. The large picture windows looked far out down Nootka Inlet, filling the room with a glorious vista of forest, cloud and distant rain.

"No more nasty chemicals!" she repeated to her cat. "No more fear that Sylvan and Esperanza are going to have their immune systems wiped out by some chemical they bump into, and end up becoming recluses in the deserts of Arizona while they try to recover. We've won, Molly. We've won!"

Molly seemed unhappy to be the recipient of such bouncy news and wriggled around anxiously until Sophie put her down. She called Max, but got stuck in his voice-mail system. She called her friend Sandra, but got a message that she had gone away skiing for a week, and Jed, would you please leave the fish in the freezer and be sure to close the back door behind you?

It was a trusting little town, Gold River, her home for the past seven years. When the pulp mill closed in 1998, some people thought it would be the end of the place, but the town had pulled together and hung on until a new wave of settlers began to arrive, attracted by its remoteness, the purity of the air and water, the low prices of the houses and the charms of the small, comfortable community.

Toxic chemicals were not an issue Sophie had thought much about until a few years ago. Her interests were more in the realms of poetry, and wildlife. Like many others, she had always sought out organic food, and tried to buy the least toxic household cleansers, but when she and her friend Sandra became pregnant at the same time, six years ago, they started reading up on things that could harm their babies. The more they read, the more alarmed they became.

"These organochlorine compounds are everywhere," Sophie said to Sandra, as they paused in their research for a morning coffee break. "They're in the pesticides and fungicides people are using in their homes and gardens; they're in fitted carpets; they're even in the treated lumber we used to build the play equipment in the park last year."

"There's a report here that says that pesticide residues have been found in eight different baby foods," Sandra replied. "You're not going to see me buying any of those, unless they're certified organic."

"And look at this," Sophie said. "It says here that Scientists at the University of California have demonstrated that rats which have been exposed to certain pesticides exhibit a higher level of aggression and irritability. Do you think this might be why the kids seem so restless these days, and unable to concentrate? It seems to me that our brains are being slowly poisoned without our knowing it."

On another occasion, Sandra had found a magazine article about something called bisphenol-A, an estrogen mimic that leaches into canned food from the plastic linings used in the tin cans. "I don't believe it," she exclaimed. "They're saying that this stuff interferes with the hormone system, and that it might be inducing 'mutagenic changes' in the next generation. What are mutagenic changes?"

"It means it affects the DNA and increases the rate of mutation. That means that *our* babies might be affected. It makes me sick!"

"It says here that concentrations of bisphenol-A found in some cans of food have twenty-seven times the amounts that cause breast cancer to proliferate in laboratory studies. No wonder there's an epidemic! What are we supposed to do? Does this mean we shouldn't eat canned foods any more?"

"And that's not all. I've read that the formaldehyde used as a bonding agent in building materials may be one of the triggers for multiple chemical sensitivity, which is affecting so many people. Now I'm worried about the glues Max is using in his canoe workshop. What if that's mutagenic too? What if his sperm have been affected, and my baby has already been damaged?"

The more Sophie and Sandra read, the more they realized that the world was being pickled in toxic chemicals, and that the regulatory agencies weren't doing their job. Out of 110,000 synthetic chemicals in use around the world, only 1,500 had ever received detailed toxicology studies. Alarmed by this information, and aided by a group called the Georgia Strait Alliance, Sophie and Sandra organized a Household De-Tox Challenge in Gold River, to see which street could reduce its use of toxic cleaning products and pesticides the most.

Everyone knew everyone in Gold River, so it didn't take long for the campaign to take off. The image of two young pregnant women fighting for the safety of their babies was irresistible to the media. They were even featured on CNN, and following the publicity, the website they had set up was inundated with inquiries from anxious parents around the world, eager to copy their example.

After they had given birth to Sylvan and Beatrice, both of whom were fine, the two women continued to campaign, widening their efforts to include the local school, and workplaces in Gold River where chemicals were used. They were not alone in their struggle. Similar campaigns were being organized all around the developed world, and the pressure was building on chemical companies and governments. In Louisiana, a group of cancer victims filed a class action suit against six chemical manufacturing companies, accusing them of withholding information which could have prevented the cancer. And in Quebec, activists picketed local garden centers, demanding that they be listed as sites contaminated with chemicals.

The beginning of the end came in June 2008, when two scientists at a university in Ontario perfected a one-day test that could be applied to any chemical (or combination of chemicals) to measure the damage it would cause to human cells, and determine whether it broke down DNA over time.

This critical information was needed to predict the potential for cancer, and events moved quickly following the announcement. Greenpeace took one hundred of the leading chemicals suspected of causing cancer, and organized a twenty-four hour marathon test by independent scientists, generating enormous media anticipation.

Sophie and Sandra had organized a special lunch party at Sandra's home to watch the results with many friends who had decided to go non-toxic. When the announcement was made, a terrific group cheer could be heard right down at the dock. Ninety-three of the chemicals tested had been shown to disrupt DNA. When she was interviewed on television, the spokeswoman for the Association of Chemical Producers responded by suggesting bias and improper scientific method, but the stock market wasn't fooled, and shares of the leading agrochemical companies had tumbled by twenty-five percent before the close of day.

Following the tests, the European Union's health standards office replicated the results, and a coalition of environmental and health groups known as Clean World established an eco-logo which began appearing on a wide variety of non-toxic cleansers, paints and other products. Greenpeace launched a worldwide Green Home Program, and in the United States, health insurance companies began offering discounts to participating families because of the reduction in harmful chemicals in their homes. Then in December 2008, an employee with Dowager Chemicals leaked documents to the *Washington Post* revealing that Dowager had known for years that some of its products caused cancer. The lawyers started to gather.

After that, it was only a matter of time. With share prices falling, class action suits accumulating and consumers abandoning products, the companies had little choice. They could either walk away from the lucrative North American and European markets and focus their energies on countries such as China and Indonesia, where the public was less informed and the corporations still controlled the regulatory process, or they could end the production and sale of the offending chemicals. Greenpeace and Clean World launched a joint campaign in China, and on May 23rd, 2009, the government of China announced that it would ban all chemicals proven to damage DNA, and would execute any Chinese citizen found smuggling, selling or otherwise distributing the chemicals. The corporations had been defeated.

Looking up from the article, Sophie gazed out at the majestic vista that gave her such pleasure. The thought that it would now be even more secure as a place to live and raise her children was deeply gratifying.

"We're safe," she whispered to Molly. "Safe at last for all generations, at least until they dream up something else."

And she burst into tears.

earthfuture

Notes

In 1999, there were approximately 75,000 synthetic chemicals in the world, of which fewer than 1,000 had been subjected to proper toxicological tests. The way the system works, a chemical is assumed innocent until proven guilty, which works to the benefit of the big corporations. The best source of information on toxics is *Rachel's Environment and Health Weekly* ($25 US per year from the Environmental Research Foundation, PO Box 5036, Annapolis, Maryland, 21403-7036, USA; erf@rachel.clark.net), especially Issue #553.

The Community De-Tox campaign which Sophie organized was modeled on one developed in 1997 by the Georgia Strait Alliance (#201, 195 Commercial Street, Nanaimo, British Columbia, V9R 5G5, Canada; (250) 753•3459; gsa@island.net).

The one-day DNA disruption test is being developed by biologist Doug Haffner and biochemist Khosrow Adeli at the Great Lakes Institute for Environmental Research, University of Windsor, Ontario, to measure the ability of contaminants to break down DNA over time. To quote Haffner, "It's a very powerful test. To be able to quantify (cell damage) — I think this is one of the first major breakthroughs dealing with the complex world of chemicals around us. It's going to cause a shift in paradigm, in what we consider to be an acceptable environment." (*Canadian Press*, April 1997)

The results anticipated in this story may begin to happen sooner than described if agreement is reached on a global treaty to phase out the use of persistent organic pollutants (POPs).

The Tides of Bold Bluff

Salt Spring Island, British Columbia
June 2009

Jack Williams awoke soon after 5 on a perfect June morning. Ever since his wife Maude died two years earlier, he had taken to getting up early to watch the sun rise and walk the dogs along the beach at Walker Hook, before digging into the day.

There was nothing in the world that could beat a quiet, sunny morning on Salt Spring Island in the summer. The ocean was so calm, he could get twenty skips when he skimmed a stone across the water. The bull kelp lazed silently off the rocks, a heron sat patiently waiting for its breakfast, and under the spreading blue of the summer's mantle, two eagles circled quietly in the sky. No one was going anywhere — except Jack, who had the biggest day of his life ahead of him.

Jack and Maude had been married for nearly forty years, until the morning she was struck down by a sudden heart attack. Their children, Clive, Pete, Hugh and Fiona, had rallied round, and so many people had gathered for the funeral they had to erect a marquee outside the tiny church where she was to be buried. Dust to dust, ashes to ashes. No words could fill the hole left by Maude's passing. Where was she now? He wished he knew.

That was the last time they had been together as a family, for Clive had taken such exception to his father's tidal turbine project that they had not spoken to each other since, and Jack had to depend on Fiona as a go-between. The fact that Clive was one of Salt Spring's newer municipal councilors made things worse, since Clive used his position to provide leadership for the project's opponents. Why was it a conflict of interest if you supported a relative's project, but not if you opposed it? Jack would never understand politics and government. He was an engineer who liked to get things done, not sit through hours of endless meetings.

Jack's project, which had caused such a storm of fascination and fury over the last three years, was to build a tidal turbine fence across a short stretch of water called Sansum Narrows. It lay between Bold Bluff Point on the island's remote western side and an area just north of Sansum Point on Vancouver Island.

The technology was relatively simple. Since water is 832 times more dense than air, a five-knot tidal current is equivalent to a 200-knot wind. Having found a location between two points where there was a strong tidal current, you inserted a number of giant turbines into the water, housed them in concrete caissons, pinned them to the ocean floor, and linked them together into a tidal fence, with a road, a series of windmills, or even a hotel on top of the structure, if you wished.

The turbines were like giant underwater windmills that turned slowly at up to twenty-five revolutions per minute, enabling the fish to swim through without being harmed. The water at Sansum Narrows was eighty meters deep, with a tidal flow of 2.4 knots at ebb, 2.1 knots at flood, providing enough thrust to make the investment financially viable. The Bold Bluff project involved twenty-five turbines, twelve on one side and thirteen on the other of a large bridged opening, which would allow the recreational boats that used the Narrows to pass through. The gap would also — and this was the heart of the controversy that had been raging ever since the project was proposed — allow the orca killer whales to pass through unharmed.

The orca whales were among British Columbia's most beloved creatures. As soon as people saw them, they fell in love with their magic, their neat black-and-white bodies, and their playful habits. A hundred years ago they lived throughout the Strait of Georgia, but today there were only thirty-five orcas left in the resident pod, which was steadily declining. Ten years earlier, they had officially been declared an endangered species. A mixture of marine pollution, zoo capture and the collapse of the salmon stocks had reduced their numbers, and now they were struggling to survive.

To Clive and the five thousand people who signed his petition to stop the project, the issue was as simple as paddling a canoe. The precautionary principle stated that if there was a risk of harming even one orca whale, it was better not to do the project. Underneath this simplicity lay a deeper ecological objection: that it was wrong to interfere with nature and her oceans. It was wrong to create a barrier across water that had flowed undisturbed through those narrows for ten thousand years. And it was wrong to change the pristine beauty of what was, Jack agreed, an exceptionally beautiful spot on the Earth.

Clive and his cohorts thought that it was wrong — but ten thousand people had signed a counter-petition in support of the project. The turbines would generate 375 megawatts of electricity, enough to provide Salt Spring with a stable source of renewable energy, with plenty left over for the local manufacture of hydrogen, using the electricity generated by the turbines to split sea-water into hydrogen and oxygen. The Island's Community Economic Trust had formed a Tidal Energy Co-operative, and its members had raised $5 million to kickstart the project. The remaining $45 million came from the British Columbia government, from the province's hydro utility in the form of a commitment to purchase fifty percent of the power, and from NASA, which wanted the hydrogen to fuel its mission to Mars.

Among the project's supporters, the excitement was infectious. The tidal fence would contribute to the clean energy revolution, which was the only hope of halting the steamroller of climate change that was causing such havoc around the world. By manufacturing hydrogen, it would create local jobs, while enabling NASA to continue its program of space exploration without spewing so many chemicals into the upper atmosphere. Fifteen marine cottages would be built on top of the fence and rented to tourists to help finance the project, and a bicycle path would be built along it, connecting Salt Spring Island to the growing network of greenways and cycle routes on Vancouver Island.

The design of the fence, with its rooftop cottages and its landscaped bicycle trail, was thought by many to be very attractive. For the killer whales, in case the gap was not enough, there would be a protective mesh on either side of the turbines, large enough to let the fish but not the orcas swim through. The orcas had been radio-tagged by marine biologists, who reported their daily progress on Orca FM 88.5 radio; there would be an underwater sonar system to alert the operator each time an orca approached; and underwater cameras would provide daylight monitoring of the turbines, so the operator could close the turbines down when a pod approached. The project was a perfect combination of sustainable technologies, Jack thought, the very thing that forward-thinking people should be supporting.

At 11 am on this gorgeous Saturday morning, the formal ground-breaking ceremony was to take place. The premier of British Columbia would be there, along with members of the Tidal Energy Co-operative, a representative from NASA, and the world's media. Greeting them, and making as much protest noise as they could in the presence of the media, would be his son Clive, with members of the Sansum Narrows Protection Society. Jack dreaded the confrontation. From the rumors he had heard, there was to be a parade of humans costumed as orca whales, an amplified poetry recital with speakers on both sides of the Narrows, and a parade of First Nations protesters claiming ancestral rights to the lands.

The approvals process could have been a lot worse. In 2004, Salt Spring Islanders had voted to incorporate, establishing their own municipal council for the first time. In the first election, in 2005, the islanders had elected a progressive slate of candidates on a platform of ecological protection, a tight control on further development, and widespread public participation. Jack's son Clive was among the new councilors.

The public participation pledge had brought exciting changes. During the summer of 2004, when southern British Columbia had baked under a relentless sun and a six-month drought, there had been a series of forest fires on the island which had caused four deaths and the loss of many homes. Coming on the heels of the massive snow-dump and the ice-storm of the previous winter, when the whole island had lost its power for three weeks, a consensus had emerged that the island needed to be organized into neighborhood clusters of twenty-five houses, and that each cluster should be fully prepared for any emergency and able to support itself. "Mr. Rogers Groups" someone called them, after the popular TV children's show about Mr. Rogers and his happy neighborhood.

The new council divided the Island into regions based on natural watersheds and set up an electoral system giving each group of thirty clusters one seat on council, ensuring that the whole island was democratically represented. Each cluster was encouraged to hold a quarterly social where people could get to know each other, and to create a Neighborhood Directory listing people's skills and resources. Working through their clusters, people were encouraged to learn about emergency preparedness, to appoint a local historian, to start the process of social and ecological mapping, and to take any concerns to a regional meeting where they could be taken up by their elected councilor. As a means of getting people to work together at the neighborhood level, the clusters had been extremely successful — and they had raised the level of debate around controversial projects like the Bold Bluff Tidal Fence.

Before embarking on the complex process of obtaining approval for the project, the Tidal Energy Co-operative had mapped out the steps it would have to take. The land on either side of the water had to be rezoned by two separate councils; they needed approvals from the federal Department of Fisheries and Oceans, the Coast Guard and various other bodies; and they would almost certainly have to undergo a full environmental assessment. It would take at least five years and cost $5 million, on top of the $5 million which had been committed for the feasibility study.

It was at this point that Fiona's partner, Dawn, made a suggestion which would make everything so much easier. Dawn was a medical doctor who combined her practice with acupuncture, reiki, and naturopathy. Ever since the outbreak of antibiotic-resistant salmonella among the Island's children five years ago, the non-drug side of her practice had been overflowing, as her patients fled the world of hospitals and orthodox medicine. She was very intuitive, and if something excited her, she supported it. That was why she wanted to help the Bold Bluffs project, she told Jack one day as they relaxed over a beer on his deck.

Why not set up a single website on the Internet, she suggested, managed by a neutral third party, and ask everyone to sign an agreement that they would share their information through the website, avoiding all the duplication and misunderstandings that would otherwise occur? The information could be arranged to make it as clear as possible, with each question positioned next to the relevant research. Unresolved issues could be tracked, and letters and petitions on either side of the argument could be published. The Co-operative followed her advice, and when the Salt Spring Council organized a public meeting before embarking on the rezoning process, they hired the same person to facilitate the debate, which speeded up the learning curve and helped to clarify the issues instead of providing a platform for myths, muddles and misleading statements, which had been the pattern for many public hearings on land rezoning in British Columbia.

So why did Clive continue to make such a noise, after approval had finally been given? The question troubled Jack immensely as he finished his breakfast, gathered his papers and set off for the opening ceremony. Clive had always had a mind of his own, long before the time he was suspended from school for slipping tablets of the drug "ecstasy" into the teachers' water cooler. He was well-known on the Island for his colorful ways, his Moroccan hats and his ability to turn a secretive and illegal income from dope into a legal income growing organic marijuana for sale to medical clinics across the USA. Only on Salt Spring could someone like Clive be elected to council, and be re-elected three years later.

Clive was by far the richest member of the family. He lived with a succession of girlfriends in an all-solar house on top of Mount Maxwell, surrounded by an electronically controlled gate to keep out intruders. Every November he disappeared for a month-long retreat into the Buddhist monastery hidden away in Salt Spring's woods. Rumor had it that Clive could have financed the entire $5 million it cost the Co-operative to start the Bold Bluff project, had he wished to.

Jack's second son, Pete, had supported the project from the start, as had his third son, Hugh, who owned a twelve-acre organic farm on the island and played an active role in the Island Growers Co-operative. Finally, there was his daughter Fiona, a writer, who tried to avoid taking sides. Jack had never been good at the comforting, cajoling and persuading that had been needed to get the siblings past their rivalries when they were growing up. It had always been Maude, their mother, who had held the family together. Without Maude, there was no center. Jack's only hope for preventing an embarrassing showdown at the ceremony was Fiona, since she and Clive had some kind of secret agreement which stemmed from the years when he had protected her against her brothers' bullying. Jack prayed that Fiona had been able to talk some sense into Clive, to prevent him from turning this morning's ceremony into a fiasco.

When Jack pulled his truck into the Bold Bluff parking area, there was plenty of activity, but no sign of Clive or the Sansum Narrows Protection Society. He walked around the corner to the site where the rocks would be blasted to clear the footings for the first turbine caisson, but still no sign of Clive. So far, so good. Fiona was there, along with Pete, Hugh, and 150 shareholders. Any minute now the premier's helicopter would be landing, carrying the NASA research chief and the ambassador from the Philippines government. The Philippines had been using the turbines successfully for several years, and the ambassador was coming to lend moral support.

At 10:45 the helicopter arrived, and they began the formal procession down to the water's edge. Still no sign of Clive. This was beginning to feel suspicious. At 10:55 the mayors of Salt Spring and North Cowichan arrived, and the cameras began to roll. Then bang on the dot of 11, just as the premier was starting her speech about the important contribution this new project would make to the development of a sustainable economy for British Columbia, they hove into view. Not one canoe, not ten, but a flotilla of fifty or more canoes, kayaks, pleasure craft and fishing smacks bearing colorful banners and flags, rounding the corner from Octopus Point in a great procession, paddling slowly against the tide. As they approached, Jack could see that in the front of each of the leading canoes there was a person dressed in full native regalia as a bear, a whale, or an eagle, waving their wings and their flippers while calling out through megaphones.

Jack's heart sank as the media cameras abandoned the speechmaking podium to focus on the arriving armada.

Suddenly another flotilla appeared from the south, bearing flags and slogans in support of the project, paddling with the tide. For a moment it looked as if the two processions would clash and there would be a marine battle fought on the water, as in olden days. Then two eagles appeared above the water, circling the scene. In First Nations culture the eagle was a bird of great spiritual significance. But to which side? Both groups paused to gaze at the eagles, and then as if at a sign, they turned to pull ashore, arriving simultaneously at the site of the ceremony. Clive's boat came to the fore and he waded ashore like some conquering emperor, dressed in a brightly colored homespun robe. He advanced to the podium. The premier's security staff moved to take control, but the premier signaled them to pause.

"Let these people be heard," she said, moving aside to let Clive take the microphone.

"We speak on behalf of the ocean," he announced in a grand oratorical style. "We speak on behalf of the salmon, and the octopus, whose lands this concrete monster will invade. We speak on behalf of the sacred orca whales, which have dwelt in these waters since time began. Let it never be said that we were silent, when they took away your home... ." — and so he continued for about five minutes.

When Clive had finished, the premier turned to the opposing armada and asked if they had anyone who would like to speak. A woman stepped out of a canoe, and came to the microphone.

"We too, have come here because we wish to speak on behalf of the ocean, the salmon and the orcas," she said. "But we hear a different message. We hear a message from the oceans all around the world, who tell us of waters where the salmon can no longer return to their spawning grounds because the sea has become too warm, where the few remaining polar bears can no longer live because their ice-floes have vanished. We too bring a message from the whales: that unless we humans stop this terrible thing that we are doing to the world's climate, they will not be here to swim through this beautiful tidal fence. They will have starved to death, and gone, they say. Build this project for us, they say, and we will willingly forego the small amount of habitat which will be lost to make way for the turbines."

Jack could hardly believe his ears. As the woman finished speaking, Clive returned to the microphone and beckoned to his father to come forward. Jack looked at the premier, but she nodded him on, so he climbed onto the rostrum.

"This is my father," Clive said to the assembled crowd. "We have not spoken directly since my mother died, two years ago. I do not like what this project represents, and we have come here to make our feelings known. But in the words of this woman who has just spoken, I also hear the voice of my mother. We too have sometimes thought those thoughts. We do not support what you are doing here, but we accept the approval you have received, and we honor the fact that you have encouraged us to speak, that the truth might prevail."

Then turning to Jack, he spoke to him personally. "I would like you to know that behind our many differences, I do admire your courage, and persistence."

He held his hand out to Jack, and embraced him. Tears ran down Jack's cheeks, and the gathered crowd applauded. Then the premier advanced to the podium, and took the microphone.

"Let the Bold Bluff tidal turbine project begin!" she cried, and the champagne bottle cracked on the rocks where the first footings would be created.

Notes

Bold Bluff is a location on Salt Spring Island which could lend itself to a tidal fence. Blue Energy is a company based in Vancouver which has developed the tidal turbine technology (**www.bluenergy.com**). At the time of writing, the Philippines government has signed an agreement to undertake feasibility studies to build a fifty-megawatt demonstration tidal turbine, graduating into a 600-megawatt project that will provide electric power to the Philippines, generating hydrogen fuel to replace the millions of propane cookers which darken Manila's skies with their pollution, emitting greenhouse gases.

Salt Spring Island has an active organic farming community, and a nascent vision of community-based economic development. It does not yet have municipal self-government.

Cobble Hills

Cobble Hills, Ontario
September 2009

Brandy could not contain the euphoria that zipped through her, in mini-explosions of exultation and disbelief. A thousand people from ecovillages all around the world were gathered right here at Cobble Hills, their own little ecovillage near the Haliburton Highlands, two hours north of Toronto. All week long they had been meeting, talking, camping and helping with tasks around the village, rounding off their days with bouts of dancing, soccer and volleyball.

As the week went by, their warmth towards each other had grown. At the start of the week, some people had found the spontaneity and humor of the North Americans a bit overwhelming, but after six days and nights of intensive workshopping, there was nothing stopping this crowd. They were set to party all night.

What had happened to turn the tiny ecovillage movement of the late twentieth century into such a roaring success? The North American office of the World Ecovillages Society (WES) had over 20,000 families and individuals waiting to move into the ecovillages that were popping up in virtually every state and province across the continent.

When Brandy and her sister Liz bought their eighty acres of farm, lake and forest at Cobble Hills, back in 2001, they thought it would be an enormous struggle to realize their vision of building an ecovillage — a small, car-free cluster of ecologically designed houses where twenty to thirty families could live a peaceful, sustainable existence, deriving their income from a mixture of organic farming, ecoforestry and home-based business activities. That was before they made the decision to hire a professional development manager, and before the media's fascination with the graphic rendering of the future village led to an onslaught of inquiries.

By 2004, they had received planning approval for 125 dwelling units, and the first residents were moving in. The magic formula which was to create such a wave of change in real estate development across North America had started to work: Find a piece of land, where possible within cycling distance of an existing settlement. Map out its ecological and soil characteristics, and design your village on one portion of it, with the houses clustered closely together. Set aside an area for common parking, enabling the village to become fully pedestrian, with attractive paths, walks, gardens, and barbecue pits for those long summer-night parties. Set aside an area as an ecological reserve, and plan a system of trails. Incorporate the best environmental features such as passive-solar architecture, environmentally sound building materials, locally generated wind, solar or ground-source energy, and solar aquatic sewage treatment, which treats the liquid wastes using aquatic plants in a series of greenhouses, turning out almost pure water. Encourage do-it-yourself building and straw-bale building techniques, and a range of flexible housing designs, some as small as 400 square feet, for single people. As far as possible, involve the future residents in the design — and make friends with the neighbors, so that they understand what you're doing. Wind your way through the approvals and rezoning process, and when you are ready, establish a local car-share co-operative so that residents can get around without having to own personal cars — and arrange a community mortgage to pay for all the shared facilities.

Two years later, the World Ecovillages Society held its annual committee get-together at Cobble Hills, and decided that it was time to win cultural acceptance for the ecovillage idea. At the time, there were approximately eighty ecovillages in North America, including cohousing projects, and they were proving very successful, both socially and financially. In market terms, they made for a good real estate prospect. WES's studies showed that in contrast to inner city or suburban life, ecovillage residents had a higher level of personal contentment, greater fulfillment, less stress and less financial worry. Their children, furthermore, showed a significantly reduced incidence of allergies, hyperactivity and attention deficit disorder. Some said it was due to the absence of chemical pesticides and chemically laden carpets, and to all the locally grown organic food they were eating. Others thought that because the ecovillages were car-free, there was a higher degree of neighbor-to-neighbor contact, giving the children a stronger support network among non-parental adults. Others put it down to the reduced use of television and videos — at Cobble Hills, there was a film every Friday night in the village hall, chosen by electronic poll and digitally downloaded from the Internet; TV was mostly limited to special occasions.

Whichever way you crunched the figures, ecovillages came out with a reduced impact on the environment, reduced carbon dioxide emissions, reduced crime, reduced personal debt-loads among the residents and increased personal satisfaction. Encouraged by these figures, WES commissioned a thorough study of the benefits of ecovillage living, and with help from a municipal lawyer, drafted a Smart Growth bill for use at the state and provincial level, offering tax incentives and streamlined approvals to development proposals which satisfied a list of social and environmental criteria, designed to encourage ecovillage-style developments. Oregon's legislators were the first to buy into the idea, seeing it as an excellent tool to control suburban sprawl. Oregon was followed by California and Washington, and then by Ontario and British Columbia. The ball was rolling.

With Smart Growth legislation on the books in a growing number of states, WES turned its attention to helping the ecovillage visionaries turn their dreams into reality. They wrote the book *Ecovillages for Dummies*, and trained people to become ecovillage development managers. By approaching the socially responsible investment funds, they established the EcoVillage Bonds, which were now the main source of development finance for most projects. Sensitive to the criticism that ecovillages were being built on former farms or forest lands, they set up a program to help existing neighborhoods acquire ecovillage characteristics, such as car-free areas, revitalized village centers, pedestrian and cycle trails, and shared neighborhood facilities.

By 2008, they were beginning to see the results. There were 165 projects on the go in North America, and ecovillages were winning increasing attention at the international level. The global need for sustainable housing was enormous, yet the normal way of planning and building was far too costly in terms of land, infrastructure and building materials. Sprawl cost taxpayers a whack of money —and the voters and politicians were beginning to realize it.

Later that year, WES put together a roadshow and took the ecovillage idea on tour to twenty developing countries, starting in Mexico and ending in China. The response was incredible. In many towns and cities, they received the kind of treatment normally given to visiting mayors. Underlying their apparent love affair with all things Western, from big hotels to junk food franchises, the nations they visited shared a deep concern about what was being lost, and the effect that western consumerism was having on their youth. Over and over, they heard the same story, in Rio, Cairo, Madras — an unsatisfied hunger for a different path of development, which could combine the best of solar and environmental technologies with a conscious remembering of local traditions. The ecovillage idea had struck a chord.

That was last year, and today, ecovillage activists from the countries they had visited were gathering here, at Cobble Hills. Brandy had never heard so many languages spoken in one place before, or seen so many people fascinated by different ways of treating sewage or organizing local currencies. She felt proud, as if they were her children. Over there in the village square they were busy partying, dancing the night away in a hundred different ethnic styles, while she stood here in the darkness, soaking up the pleasure under the million shining stars of a warm Ontario September night. This was a night that made all the struggles and uncertainties worthwhile; this was truly a night to remember.

Notes

In 1999, there were approximately fifty ecovillages and cohousing projects in North America (with others in Europe and Australasia). Cohousing projects are designed by their members, and include a common house for shared cooking and eating, in a pedestrian, car-free environment. Ecovillages are similar, and try to achieve greater self-sufficiency in energy and food production. Smart Growth legislation is increasingly being adopted by state legislatures in the USA, in an attempt to limit sprawl. Brandy is a friend who is establishing a real ecovillage on Vancouver Island.

For more information, check out:

- Global EcoVillages Network **www.gaia.org**
- Global EcoVillages Europe, Declan Kennedy, Lebensgarten, Ginsterweg 5, D-31595, Steyerberg, Germany; (+49) 5764 93040; even@lebensgarten.gaia.org
- Global EcoVillage Network (Oceania), Max Lindegger, MS 16, Lot 59, Crystal Waters, Queensland 4552, Australia; (+61) 7 5494 4741; lindegger@gen-oceania.org; **www.gaia.org/thegen/genoceania**
- EcoVillage Network of Canada, RR 2, Cameron, Ontario, K0M 1G0, Canada; (705) 887·1553; sunrun@lindsaycomp.on.ca
- EcoVillage Network of the Americas, 556 Farm Road, PO Box 69, Summertown, Tennessee, 38483-0090, USA; (615) 964·4324; ecovillage@thefarm.org
- *Better NOT Bigger: How to Take Control of Urban Growth and Improve Your Community*, by Eben V. Fodor (New Society Publishers, 1999).

The Dawning of the Solar Age

Berlin, Germany
August 2010

Mimi lay back on her bed and watched the sun pour in through the window of the third-floor apartment in Berlin that she shared with Hans. Out on the balcony the window boxes were full of deep blue lobelia and red geraniums, and her thick, juicy tomatoes were soaking up the heat. They loved it out there, sun-trapped in their urban home.

Mimi still found it a struggle, coming to terms with the fact that this would probably be her last summer on Earth. These would be the last months she would gaze onto the incredible, ethereal blue of the summer sky, probably clearer than she'd ever known it now that the air pollution was reduced; the last summer when she would follow the dance of the swallows between the rooflines. Thirty-seven years she'd had, to enjoy this thing called life.

The latest strain of drug-resistant tuberculosis had gotten into her lungs. She had probably caught it among the street people, many of whom were active in the solar movement. With no drugs to control its virulence, it was only a matter of months before she coughed one last time and left this beautiful world forever. She could no longer listen to Kurt Weill or Edith Piaf — they were too alive for the bitter-sweet melancholia that filled her soul. Debussy, Ravel, and Beethoven's final quartets — these were her choice of music these days.

From five floors above, Mimi could hear the occasional thud of a hammer as the housing co-operative's work crew installed the solar shingles. By waiting until they had signed up 400 houses, they had negotiated a fifteen percent discount on the price, sufficient to win consensus within the co-op. It was great that the Solar Fund was there to provide the financing, no questions asked.

It had been back in 2002 that Mimi had first proposed adding solar cladding to the roofs of the three apartment buildings that made up their co-op. Since then the price had fallen from 40,000 deutschemarks to 6,000 for a typical 800-square-foot apartment. To think that as recently as the mid-1990s, it cost closer to DM 100,000. That was around the time when Mimi had first grasped the danger that climate change posed to the planet, and started looking for alternatives.

Sometime next spring, ten percent of Germany's energy would come from renewable energy. Mimi knew she might not be around to see it happen, but she could anticipate the celebrations. Ten percent by 2010 meant that Germany was on target for the end of fossil fuel use by 2025. If the rest of the world matched their progress, it would mean an earlier stabilization of the planet's troubled atmosphere and a gradual reduction in the terrible storms, floods, droughts, hurricanes and forest fires that had been devastating the world. With solar, wind and other renewable energies increasing their share of the market by twenty percent a year for the last eight years, the hundred percent target had been officially recognized as reachable. Denmark had reached ten percent as far back as 2002, thanks to the offshore windfarms and the wind turbines that the farmers' co-operatives had been installing all over the country.

The Netherlands was next: they hit their target in 2008, following an all-out drive by the Economic Affairs Ministry to make renewable energy the driving force behind the country's economic development. Thanks to government support, Dutch wind turbines were generating energy from Chile to China, earning good money for Dutch businesses. They'd had the smarts to see where the future lay at a time when the United States and Canada were still subsidizing the oil, gas and coal industries. As recently as the year 2000, Mimi recalled, the world's governments were giving the fossil-fuel industry the unbelievable sum of $650 billion a year of taxpayers' money — $74 million every hour, twenty-four hours a day. It was good that those days were over, she thought.

She hoped Hans would be home soon. When she recalled the work they had done together over the past seven years, she felt so grateful to have had a partner who supported her enthusiasm. She was so vulnerable these days, emotionally. A tear slipped down her cheek, and she was assaulted by another wave of the awful coughing, and the bloody mucous that her body threw up in its vain attempt to reject the disease that had taken up residence in her lungs.

Hans was a poet, a wild, crazy poet whose thick black hair stood up on end. Mimi used to say he must be receiving a constant shockwave of energy from the gods for it to stay that way. Only in Berlin, Mimi thought, could people like Hans be accepted and earn a decent living from their craziness. By contrast, Mimi was small, petite and dark, scarcely more than five feet tall — but filled with a love of music and a devotion to the planet and everything that lived on it. Her father said there must have been some Jewish or gypsy blood in the family, which had somehow escaped Hitler's obsession with purity.

Hans's specialty was organizing huge, colorful, outdoor spectacles, often involving thousands of people. The day they met, Midsummer's Day 2003, he was conducting a choir of fifty people on top of the Brandenburg Gate at dawn, showering Berlin with a chorus of the most heavenly, breathtaking harmonies. That was typical Hans.

So when Hans fell passionately in love with Mimi, he soon applied his imagination to her work with *der Gesselschaft für Alternativen Energien*, Berlin's Society for Green Energy. In 2005 they organized Berlin's Festival of the Sun together, as a celebration of solar and renewable energy. There was a solar challenge to find the street which boasted the most solar houses; a solar car race; and a visit by the Sun-Raycer, the solar airplane that had just completed its first voyage around the world. In parks and on roof-tops around the city, Hans installed unique solar music instruments fitted with electronic sensors, which vibrated with different tubular harmonies each time the temperature increased or fell by a degree. Mimi smiled as she recalled the frustration he went through, trying to make it work.

The following year, the Society for Green Energy had dreamed up the idea of awarding Green Stars to individuals whose homes were completely powered by renewable energy, who did not drive a fossil fuel powered vehicle, and who took no air flights during the year. Mimi and Hans had been among the first recipients. They cycled wherever they went; they refused to fly because of the damage planes did to the atmosphere; and the passive-solar house where they used to live in Magdeburg was so energy-efficient it only needed 2 kW solar modules for all its energy needs. By 2008, there were 135,000 Green Star recipients in Germany, and the badge was seen as the ultimate symbol of "cool" by the younger generation. The only rule was that you had to have a home to live in. The homeless could not apply, the Society decided, a decision which caused huge internal arguments. One side said that it would degrade the Green Stars to give them to people just because they were destitute, and could not afford to use fossil fuel energy. The other side said that excluding the homeless would make the Stars just another bourgeois invention designed to oppress the poor.

It had been Hans's idea to apply a similar rating system to Germany's politicians, at the state and federal levels. The Society established a ten-point rating system covering their homes, their means of transport, and the number of flights they took each year. The results were a huge embarrassment for some of Germany's highest ranking politicians, who scored zero. To an increasing number of Germans, personal lifestyle sustainability was one of the most important social values of the early twenty-first century.

Mimi wondered where Hans was, and what he was doing. She had become much more dependent on his love since contracting TB, which kept her in isolation because of its infectious nature. Only Hans, her nurse and a few close friends were allowed to see her, and they had to undergo weekly contagion tests. Sometimes she wondered if she could trust him when he was away. She knew that other women found him attractive, but what could she offer him? The passion had long since flown from her poor defeated body, which he used to love so much. She wouldn't blame him if he were secretly finding his pleasure elsewhere — but she couldn't bear the thought of losing his love to someone else. Not yet, please God, not yet. Not until she was gone.

In Hans's absence, Mimi spent long hours on her own with just the company of her black cat, Theophilus, and the occasional look-in from her painter friend Elke, who lived on the floor above. Thanks to the Internet, she was able to maintain a lively contact with friends and colleagues around the world. Some people didn't like video-mail, preferring old-fashioned e-mail, but to Mimi, the ability to see the faces of her friends as they talked was a very wonderful thing. She also received greetings from some of the world's solar leaders, who knew her personally from her years of involvement in the solar movement, and made a point of pausing in their days to call and say hello.

Like most people, Mimi received her news through the specialized Internet news services she subscribed to, which she downloaded onto her handheld electronic tablet. This was how she maintained her phenomenal knowledge of the solar revolution. She knew how close Crete was to becoming the world's first completely solar island, thanks to the solar power plants constructed with Greenpeace's assistance. She knew about the huge tidal turbines that had been installed in the Philippines, capturing the energy that surged back and forth between the islands. She knew about the progress Iceland was making towards becoming a hydrogen-based economy, manufacturing hydrogen with hydroelectric, geothermal and wind energy, and shipping the surplus to Germany to supply the growing number of refuelling stations. In her own neighborhood, the Berlin car-share co-operative operated a fleet of small hydrogen-powered city-cars. As soon as the co-op's solar roof was finished, they were going to install a fuel cell in the basement, and use the surplus energy from the roof to make hydrogen for the cars. Mimi loved this kind of closed-loop economy. It was true, they were just one small apartment in a world that was still full of gas-guzzling vehicles, but you had to start somewhere. Everything had to start somewhere.

Some of the developments she read about were truly mind-boggling. In Geneva, Swiss engineers were busy pioneering the world's first solar road. They had paved a road with solarvoltaic cells, and then covered it with an ultra-durable transparent surfacing material. Just imagine, she thought — every road on the planet becoming a solar generator! In Japan, the research scientists at Sanyota had developed a high quality solar enamel, using nanotechnology (the technology of ultra-tiny things) to create tiny fibrous electronic links between trillions of nanosolar cells, which were then mixed into the paint, enabling the entire painted surface of a building, a car, an airplane or an ocean liner to generate solar energy. Looking down the road, scientists were talking about the time when every manufactured surface in the world could be treated with a nanosolar coating. People said nanosolar energy was the hottest thing to invest in, but so far, the Solar Fund was holding back, awaiting more results.

Mimi lay on her bed, watching the sun move through the sky until the evening's shadows began to fall over Berlin. Their street had been converted into a pedestrian area ten years ago, and she enjoyed the filtered sounds of conversations, bicycle bells and children playing that drifted up through the lime trees.

And then there were the Arab countries, which had been holding up the global greenhouse gas negotiations for so long. Together with the United States, they formed a substantial barrier to progress, since the countries depended on the sale of oil for so much of their income, and found it hard to change their perspective. It was one of the greatest paradoxes of the early twenty-first century that it should be countries such as the Netherlands and Germany, in relatively cloudy northerly latitudes, that were pioneering the solar revolution, while the countries of the Middle East, which baked in year-round sun, were resisting it. Everyone knew that the world's oil supply was diminishing, but with oil-prices so high, it was hard for the oil-producing countries to think beyond the current bonanza.

In 2006, while Mimi was still living the hectic life of a global solar activist, she had been invited by the King of Jordan to speak at a meeting of Arab princes and rulers in Amman. Travelling by sea from Trieste to Tel Aviv, then overland to Jordan, she had time to read up on the troubled history of the Middle East and OPEC before entering this difficult and complex world, of which she knew so little. She also took the time to seek guidance from the sun and the ocean, which she did whenever she embarked on a difficult quest.

The meeting seemed to go well, and during the voyage home, after a brief holiday in Israel, she had reflected on the two days she had spent among the princes, kings and dictators. Apart from a handmaid given to her by the Queen to look after her needs, she was the only woman in a sea of black-and-white-robed men. It was clear from the start that some of the assembled rulers resented her presence, but the King of Jordan made up for it by his kindness. Her presentation of solar, wind and tidal developments around the world had been received in silence. She had gone on to talk about the way in which Danish, Dutch, German and Japanese companies had been able to steal a commanding lead on the USA, thanks to the progressive policies of their governments. Then she had shown a series of images which told the history of fuels, going right back to firewood and the rise of coal, showing that there were very few years remaining in which oil would be the prime source of energy for the world. The new wave of renewable energies had achieved a momentum that was unstoppable. The only decision remaining for an oil-producing country was whether to make the shift to the solar revolution now, or wait until the last drop was gone.

After her presentation, while she stood waiting for the taxi to take her to the bus station, the King of Jordan had come out in person, kissed her on the hand in a very gracious manner, and thanked her for her contribution. "You did very well, my dear," he said. "You did very well." Later, the Society received a check for DM 50,000, with a personal thank-you note from the King.

She would never know what transpired during the rest of the meeting, but six months later there was an announcement that the Arab states were forming a consortium with the Japanese mega-corporation, Sanyota. Together, they would turn the sun-baked deserts of the Middle East into an ocean of solar farms, providing electricity for the entire region, and using the surplus energy to manufacture hydrogen from sea-water on a massive scale, shipping it around the world in converted pipelines and tankers. It was a partnership made in heaven. The Arab nations would provide the land and the pipeline infrastructure, while Sanyota would provide the solar expertise and access to the world hydrogen market to fuel the hydrogen-powered automobiles they were manufacturing.

Across the Atlantic in Washington, Congress was in shock. In the brief moment that it took to make the announcement, the United States lost a critical piece of its national security strategy. Heads rolled in the Department of Energy and the CIA, as the American media tore into the US government. "How could things have gone so wrong?" they demanded to know. "How could the Japanese have stolen what was thought to have been America's most crucial global asset?"

Of all the things I have done in my life, Mimi thought to herself now, that meeting in Amman was probably the most influential. She had never informed the German media of her visit; she had known instinctively that it was one of those private affairs which was not to be disclosed. Only Hans and a few of her closest friends had known.

As the sun left the balcony, Theophilus came in from the spot where he had been soaking up its warmth and jumped onto her bed. It was only four years since that historic trip, and yet all across the Middle East and North Africa, from Libya to Iran, the solar collectors were under construction. European companies had been quick to follow Sanyota's trail, setting up new partnerships, while America seemed more obsessed with breaking the Arab-Japanese connection than in making a serious effort to join the game.

"It's all so exhausting, trying to understand the politics of the world," Mimi said to Theophilus, stroking his silky black fur. "What did I ever know of all that? Sometimes, Theophilus, I think there is a whole other level, where the really big decisions get made, away from the arguing and the deals. A level that exists within the hearts and minds of quiet people around the world, known and unknown, encouraged by the prayers of millions. I wouldn't put it past you, Theophilus, to be in on that level. Let the humans think they are running the world: but all the while, it's really you and your cohorts. Is that why you came to live with me? To be my guardian angel? I wouldn't put it past you." Theophilus just lay there and purred.

Later that evening, after the sun had left Berlin to greet a new day in China, Hans came home bearing freshly baked bread, red wine and a basket full of plums. Mimi didn't ask where he'd been — she was just happy to see him with his mop of crazy hair. He kissed her, opened the wine, and sat on her bed. She rested her head on his chest while he told her of the day's events. Mimi no longer took in all the details; she just enjoyed his energy, and his presence. What a strange and curious world it was, she thought, that humans could send a mission to Mars, create living clones of a tiger and cover large parts of the desert in solar arrays, and yet not be able to deal with this tiny microbe that was slowly eating away her life.

"I shall come back as a cat," she announced to Hans as he was in the middle of describing the moving wall of poetry he was working on, which would float through the streets of Berlin on silken sheets. Hans stopped in mid-sentence to take in what Mimi was saying.

"I shall come back as a cat," she repeated, and in her mind, she pictured herself as Hans's cat, a huge, strong, ginger cat, silently helping him in his work, while growling at his girlfriends. "I think that's how the world works, you know. *Ist eine katzenregierung.* A government by cats. We just think we're the ones who are doing it."

"I sometimes wonder about you, Mimi," Hans replied affectionately. "Is this what you want me to tell the volunteers at the Society for Green Energy when they ask about you? That you are turning into a feline mystic, who spends her day meditating on cats?"

"Whatever you like, Hans," she said. "I think we've won. I think from now on, the solar age is inevitable. So maybe I'm entitled to spend my days thinking about higher things."

Whereupon Theophilus looked at her, and purred some more.

Notes

Solar power is the world's second fastest growing energy source, after wind. Sales of solarvoltaic cells around the world have been increasing at an average sixteen percent per year since 1990, ten times the rate of the oil industry. Shipments of solarvoltaic cells increased by twenty-one percent between 1997 and 1998. In 1998, there were 800 megawatts of solar energy in place globally — less than one percent of the global power supply, but growing fast. Scientists believe that the new generation of thin-film solar cells will cut the cost from $4 to $1 per watt by 2008, making them competitive in many parts of the world. Some suggest that solarvoltaic roofing shingles will fall to a reasonable price by 2004. A typical small solar rooftop system will prevent the burning of more than seven tonnes of coal in its lifetime, or the creation of almost one hundred kilograms of nuclear waste.

Domestic hydrogen fuel cell units are already available. By 1999, Denmark's wind industry was producing eight percent of the country's energy. The Netherlands has set a target of achieving ten percent of its energy from renewable sources by 2010, aided by the Economic Affairs Ministry. The developments in Crete, the Philippines and Iceland are all happening today. For an overview of the global solutions to climate change which are available today, see **www.davidsuzuki.org/energy**.

The solar roads, solar paint and nanosolar technology are speculative, as are the developments between the Arab nations and Sanyota.

Recommended reading:

- *Solar Today* magazine, American Solar Energy Society, 2400 Central Avenue, Suite G-1, Boulder, Colorado, 80301, USA; (303) 443•3130; Fax (303) 443•3212; ases@ases.org
- *The Real Goods Solar Source Catalog*, 555 Leslie Street, Ukiah, California, 95482-5576, USA; Fax (707) 468•9846; realgoods@realgoods.com
- *The Sunshine Revolution* by Harald N. Røstvik is available for $39 US plus postage from Sun Lab, Alexander Kiellandsgt. 2, 4009 Stavanger, Norway; Fax (47) 51 52 40 62. A very beautiful, inspiring book.
- *From Space to Earth: The Story of Solar Electricity* by John Perlin is available from aatec publications, PO Box 7119, Ann Arbor, Michigan, 48107, USA; (800) 995•1470; aatec@aol.com

I'm Dreaming
of a Green Christmas...

December 2010

Dear Emily,

I've been pondering this letter for some time, letting my mind wander as I sit by the fire.

I'm approaching seventy and you're just seventeen, about to step into the world, and there's something about Christmas and the midwinter season that I want to catch, while it's in my mind.

Some years ago, when the environmental movement was beginning to reject consumerism in a big way, many people decided to do away with material gifts altogether — at least those that were mass produced. There was a feeling that our precious midwinter season had been stolen and colonized, that our very souls were viewed as vacant territory to be occupied and subdued by the corporations and their merchants. As we grew to understand the true ecological impact of these "gifts" — the forests that were being torn down, the rivers filled with waste, the lungs of factory workers filled with chemicals — the whole affair began to feel sickening.

What had happened to the magic? Was this what it meant, that our lust for material satisfaction should be bought at such cost? Was this what we wanted for Christmas?

So one year we decided to do a completely green Christmas. No material gifts at all, we said, unless they were made by hand, so we hid ourselves away in the corners of the house, making things for each other. It was delightful. That was the year your grandmother made the quilt we all love so much, the year we collected your childhood photos and paintings and put them together in the album you treasure.

Your dad was working right up to Christmas night that year, and he complained that he had no time to make anything. He liked the green Christmas idea, but the closer it got, the more he was tempted to rush out and buy things for us all.

In the end, he started a whole new tradition. He put together books of personal vouchers which we could cash in whenever we liked for a trip to the theatre, an undisturbed day of his time, a mystery breakfast, a full-body massage or a weekend's house-sitting — things like that. His vouchers were such a hit that in the years that followed we started to dream up more and more imaginative gifts — I still recall the mystery tour your mother gave us once, when we had no idea that we would end up in the Empress Hotel being serenaded by carolers.

So what is it that I really want to say? Since making that decision all those years ago, we have become quite expert at creating our own gifts. After a few years of abandoning commercial gifts, however, we decided to relax the rules a little bit, and agreed that we could give each other one small store-bought gift, as well as the home made gifts and vouchers.

It was then that I realized the subtle way in which advertising and commercial pressure seek to colonize our hearts and desensitize them, with their insistent demand to buy, just as a drug pusher does. After the years of carefully tuning in to create the perfect gifts, seeking that special something that would touch your soul, going back to the shops felt like returning to an old addiction. It was so easy to opt for a quickly chosen "thing"; it takes such determination to apply the intimacy of the caring spirit to shopping in the big consumer stores, where they are trying so hard to push their stuff, to overwhelm your sensitivity. Thank heaven for the small, owner-operated stores, where the owners have found a way to integrate their spirit with their merchandise, where you know from the moment you walk in that you are in a special place, beyond commercialism.

It was then that I saw what had happened. Our ability to give intimately had been colonized and destroyed by commercialism — in some families, taken over completely. Reclaiming it takes care, but it's so worth the effort. The more care and love you put into choosing a gift, whatever its source, the more alive it will be.

Christmas, midwinter, the solstice — it's a time of rebirth, when we celebrate the light at the heart of winter, through candles, stars, and the love that is rekindled by giving and being together. If you let the stores colonize your heart, and replace the personal act of giving with the commercial desire simply to find a "gift," the process of rekindling will be that much weaker, and your family will be the poorer.

I didn't realize this when I started out; it is a very profound thing that I'm talking about. The commercialism of the stores seems so normal, but in fact it is an invasion, an invasion of our hearts that, unless we maintain a constant vigil, can steal away our ability to give simply and lovingly.

This has been a long sermon from an elderly grandpa, but I hope you will understand, and forgive me for it.

Happy Christmas, my dearest Emily,
from Grandpa Joe

Hamlet's Ode
to the 21st Century

To grow, or not to grow: that is the question:
Whether 'tis nobler on the Earth to suffer
The filth and waste of outrageous production
Or to take arms against a toxic sea of troubles,
and by opposing, end them? To breathe: to pause:
To look anew; and by this pause to say we end
The heartache and ten thousand unnatural shocks
That Earth is heir to, 'tis a consummation
Devoutly to be wish'd. To breathe, to pause;
To pause: perchance to dream: ay, there's the hope;
For in that breath of hope what dreams may come
When we have shuffled off this monstrous myth,
Must give us pause; there's the nub
That makes a dread of so much hope;
For who would bear the poisons and foul stench of growth,
The oppressor's wrong, the proud industrialist's contumely,
The pangs of Gaia's wounds, the law's delay,
The insolence of office and the spurns
That Nature so unworthily takes,
When we ourselves might Earth-love make
With a bare choice? Who would sorrows bear
To choke and die a cancerous life,
But that the dread of life without the car,
The undiscovered country in whose bourn
Our dreams might live, puzzles the will
And makes us rather bear those ills we have
Than fly to others that we know not of?

Thus dross materialism makes cowards of us all;
And thus the native hue of resolution
Is sicklied o'er with the pale cast of greed,
And enterprises far beyond the goals of "more!"
and "more!" with this regard their currents turn awry,
And lose the name of action.

With apologies to William Shakespeare

Outbreak!

Glasgow, Scotland
December 2004

It was Christmas morning when the first signs of trouble hit. The Royal Infirmary in Glasgow, Scotland, reported an "unusual incidence" of streptococcus bacteria that was "not responding to treatment." When Hugh McCann from the *Herald* called to speak to someone from the hospital, he was put on to a rather tetchy administrator who muttered something about the "bloody media" before he put on his official voice and said, "There is really nothing to worry about — we'll call you if there's a problem. It's just a common bug. We're dealing with them all the time," and then hung up.

"You can tell he's not been to media training school," Hugh laughed, and sent a "patient" round to see what she could dig up.

Later that evening, Fiona McQuarry called on her cellular phone from inside the hospital. "It's absolutely nuts in here!" she whispered, clearly afraid someone would overhear her. "I still can't find out what it is, but they've got six wards completely sealed off, they've cut the phones to those wards, and as far as I can tell they're confiscating everyone's cell phones, saying the signals interfere with open-heart surgery. It's bullshit. As far as I can tell, they're panicking. There's been some kind of an outbreak — they're cleaning and scrubbing absolutely everywhere. The younger nurses are shit-scared. All leave's been cancelled, and they've got heavy security on all the doors — male orderlies, big and important. Whatever it is, it's got me freaked. You never told me it was this kind of assignment. I've got young kids at home, and I want to see them — now. Got to stop — someone's coming. I'll call later."

The next morning the *Herald* ran a deliberately small story on the front page: "Hospital Sealed Off: Staff Say Nothing to Worry About." Within hours the hospital was surrounded by crowds demanding to know what was happening to the relatives, friends and lovers who were locked inside. The police sealed off all the streets leading to the hospital, and the Minister for Health was forced to go on the air to reassure the public that while the hospital was having a small problem with an unusually stubborn bacteria, it was nothing that a good dose of the right antibiotic would not sort out. Yes, she announced, there had been three deaths, but it was a large hospital full of sick people, and there was nothing abnormal about that.

Inside the hospital, it was entirely another story. "So what the hell ARE we supposed to tell them?" a senior consultant was shouting. "That we've got this strep bug that is killing one patient in ten, and we've got nothing on it? That the fuckin' bug is out of control? And have the patients storming the doors, carrying the wretched thing all over Glasgow? Don't be mad, man — we've GOT to contain it, even if it means lying through our teeth."

No force on Earth could have kept the doors sealed. The hospital staff had thrown every last antibiotic in the book at it, and the bacteria kept on multiplying. By the end of the second day they had lost a hundred patients, and the orderlies guarding the rear entrance had run for it. Their escape was kept secret, but within three days, two other hospitals were fighting the same bacteria.

It was then that the Scottish Minister for Health made her historic broadcast:

I am afraid I have to announce that the outbreak of strep bacteria in Glasgow's Royal Infirmary is far more serious than we had anticipated. Three hundred and twenty-three people have died so far, and the country is in its worst public health crisis since the flu epidemic following World War One. Our government is taking the unprecedented step of closing every hospital in the city, both public and private, since the bug seems to have found a way to spread from hospital to hospital. Small emergency clinics are being set up in civic centers as I speak. You might think this an extreme course of action, but in the current situation, we have decided it is the wisest course. We must bear the immediate pain to minimize the risk of any more bacteria escaping, causing more widespread pain later. All patients will be cared for, and emergency hotlines have been set up for every hospital region in the country. We are in a very unpleasant and difficult situation. Let us share the anxiety and pray together, each as we see fit. Our greatest sympathy and respect goes out to those who have lost loved ones. With courage, we will overcome this crisis. Thank you for listening.

Within medical circles, they had been expecting the outbreak for years. The Chairwoman of the British Medical Association sent a letter to the *Times*, in which she wrote:

It's amazing it took this long. The bacteria can evolve far faster than we can invent new antibiotics, and every time we overuse the antibiotics, we invite the bacteria to develop a mutant strain that is resistant. It's a battle we can never hope to win. We've been playing a mug's game for the past fifty years, hoping we could trick nature with science: but nature's far smarter than we are — probably than we ever will be. It takes us seven years to develop a new antibiotic. How long does nature need to evolve a resistant strain — a few months? We'd do better if we worked on ways to join her, rather than trying to defeat her.

For a few days people behaved with remarkable tranquillity, recalling how their grandparents had lived through the war with the bombs falling all around them. By January 3rd, however, when people started returning to work after Hogmanay and the New Year's break, people began phoning in sick from work, and overnight, the crisis went from bad to appalling. The scientists' best guess was that there were some "carriers" at large in the community who were resistant to the bacteria. At first people improvised all kinds of protective masks, but then they simply shut themselves up in their homes. The non-electronic economy ground to a halt, share prices tumbled, and the pound sterling lost ten percent in the course of a single day. As the news reported the growing death toll, radio and TV talk-shows ran phone-ins and the Internet buzzed with connections from all over the world, giving people a lifeline to others.

When desperation fills the air, people open their minds to all sorts of ideas and possibilities they would normally never think about. It didn't take long for people to grasp the basic science of what was happening, nor did it take long for the voice of conventional medicine, urging patience and trust, to be drowned out by alternative practitioners and healers phoning in to explain that it was the immune system that people had to focus on, not the drugs.

"For medical science," they explained, "it has always been easier to deal with sicknesses through drugs and other kinds of direct intervention than to try to understand the incredible complexity of the human immune system. But at the end of the day, it is the immune system that protects us and keeps us healthy. When our immune systems are weak, we get sick. When they are strong, we don't. Allowing for some simplification, it's as basic as that."

As the turnaround took place in people's minds, attention turned to the variety of alternative remedies that strengthened the immune system. Over the Internet, radio, TV and telephone, people discussed the latest details they had heard about herbalism, homeopathy, natural healing, diet or group prayer. Remedies that people had never heard of before, such as "germanium," and terms like "probiotics" became common household names. The shares of big drug companies collapsed, and a small center that taught an ancient Vedic system of pranic healing found itself giving daily tuition over national television. When a Canadian company announced that it was selling shares in biofeedback equipment that enabled people to monitor the health of their own immune systems, there was a rush to buy. Holistic practitioners kept reminding people that personal attitude was the single most important component of immune system health, and that love, laughter and touch were the best healers going, but people found it hard to let go of the idea that there might still be a magic pill or potion. In spite of the obvious risk, people wearing protective masks began to gather outside the homes of every healer, herbalist or naturopath whose work was discussed on the Internet, and many of the practitioners had to hire security guards to keep order among the queues by night and day.

At the end of January, the death toll unexpectedly dropped, and within a week no new cases were being reported. The medical authorities reported that "the outbreak is now under control," but they had no idea why the bacteria had suddenly lost its will to live. Two months after the outbreak ended, an alternative health magazine ran an interview with a healer living in South London who claimed that she deliberately contracted the bug towards the end of January and had wrestled with it on the psychic level for three days, protected by a circle of spiritual supporters. She said that she had finally defeated it, but the story was never picked up by the mainstream media or the medical press.

In the wake of the outbreak, medical schools started developing programs to teach immune system analysis as a standard diagnostic tool, using a combination of biofeedback and other sensory systems. Private insurance companies began requiring clients to sign onto positive health plans that emphasized such things as diet, attitude, exercise, social involvement and personal fulfillment. Apologists for the old school of medicine called it "psycho-socialism," but for the insurance companies, it was just sound business.

The strongest opposition to the new approach came not from the medical establishment, but from scientists who refused to accept that prayer, pranic healing or the power of laughter could have any possible value, in spite of studies demonstrating their validity. In private, some were heard to admit that it wasn't so much the data that troubled them, as the lack of a unifying theory that would enable them to place the data within an acceptable paradigm.

The final death toll was 4,532 people — about the same number as died in road accidents in Britain every year, one journalist reported. One of the victims was the journalist Fiona McQuarry, who never got home to see her children. She contracted the bug a day after being locked into the hospital, and died a week later.

Notes

First published in *Medical Marriage: The New Partnership Between Orthodox and Complementary Medicine*, ed. Cornelia Featherstone & Lori Forsyth (Findhorn Press, 1997).

Three months after I wrote this story, a friend in Britain (Keith Hudson) watched the BBC TV program *Panorama* (January 15th 1996), which opened with the words "There are bacteria resistant to antibiotics spreading out of control in UK hospitals." A twenty-nine-year-old man came in after a motorbike accident, picked up an infection which antibiotics couldn't control, and died within two weeks.

The bug in the British hospitals is called MRSA — methicillin resistant staphylococci aureus — which is resistant to almost all of the present repertoire of antibiotics. "Most hospitals in the UK are now infected with MRSA.... The World Health Organization says officially that MRSA is now an epidemic. MRSA is beginning to colonize old people homes in UK and many other places where there are ill people.... Dr Michael Zeckel (US epidemiologist, Eli Lilley Laboratories) said that MRSA produces forty-eight generations in twenty-four hours — that is, 2,000 times faster than the body can produce defenses. MRSA is now resistant to almost all antibiotics except the strongest one or two, such as vancomycin." (*Panorama*)

The bigger threat is VRE — Vancomycin resistant enterococcus, which is resistant to all known antibiotics. Dr. Barry Cookson, head of UK Epidemiological Laboratory Services, says, "This is the most serious thing I have ever known or heard about. VRE can almost be described as 'clever.' It is incredible. It is awesome. As soon as a new antibiotic is used, VRE mutates resistance to it. The more new antibiotics that are produced, the more dangerous the situation becomes. It is only a matter of time before VRE infects all hospitals." Dr Rosamund Cox added, "In ten years' time we will look back on the 1980s and 1990s as a glorious time because we still had some antibiotics left that overcame bacterial infections." And Dr Matthew Scott, senior UK epidemiologist, said, "There is no new drug on the horizon: only variations of existing antibiotics to which VRE will adapt quickly. VRE is truly the Doomsday Bug."

In May 1999 the *New England Journal of Medicine* reported a type of salmonella called DT104 which had become resistant to five common antibiotics — ampicillin, chloramphenicol, streptomycin, sulfonamides and tetracycline. Donella Meadows wrote, "In 1980 antibiotic-resistant DT104 showed up in less than one percent of samples tested at the Center for Disease Control. Now it shows up in thirty-four percent. It is even more widespread in England, where some strains show resistance to six or seven antibiotics."

In June 1999 Canada's *Globe and Mail* ran the cover story "Deadly superbugs plague Canada's hospitals." It reported that in 1998 in Ontario, MRSA resulted in 8,100 cases, 1,000 infections and an estimated fifty to one hundred deaths. The incidence of MRSA had risen from under 250 cases in 1994 to 8,000 in 1998. In 1995 the Toronto Hospital recorded Canada's first outbreak of VRE. By 1998 they were admitting one new VRE patient every forty-five days, mainly snowbirds returning from Florida, where VRE had become widespread. VRE is not a killer, but "the fear is that VRE will pass its vancomycin genes to the more virulent MRSA, which could thrust medicine back to the pre-penicillin days." In the 1970s, when there were 25,000 antibiotics on the market, many of the world's diseases appeared to be practically eradicated, so the drug companies lost interest in trying to kill germs. They are now scrambling to re-assemble their microbial experience, but it takes an average of ten years to bring a new drug to market. VRE has its origins among European farmers who fed antibiotics to their livestock as a growth promoter during the 1970s and 1980s. "VRE turned up in animal carcasses, and [then in] workers who toiled amid moist bits in the abattoirs. Then it slipped into the human food chain in steak, chicken and bacon." (*Globe & Mail*)

The human attempt to outwit nature may turn out to be a losing game: we might do better to learn more about our own innate healing abilities, and how to live alongside her.

Stop Press: As this book was on its way to press, the *Guardian Weekly* (Sep 9 -15, 1999) ran a story headed "Alarm as superbug hits British hospitals," which described the discovery of two cases of a new superbug called Visa which had evolved to resist vancomycin, accelerating fears that medicine could be facing a return to the pre-penicillin days when all surgery carried the risk of infection and death. The cases were found at the Glasgow Infirmary ....

The Pangs of Gaia's Wounds

Sundareya, Orissa, India
May 2011

Kerry stared at her child's tiny, misshapen sex organ with a sick feeling in her stomach. She loved Dana unreservedly, but the sick feeling had not diminished in the six months since she had given birth. There seemed to be a kind of clitoris growing half inside, half on top of the penis. She would have assumed it to be some kind of genetic error, except that hers was the fourth such child she had seen in the last two years. It gave her a feeling that something was going terribly wrong.

She and Lars had traveled to India as volunteers twenty years ago, she from Connemara, in Ireland, he from Denmark. They met while hiking the foothills of the Himalayas, and fell in love when they met again in the small village of Sundareya, in southern Bihar. It was a village like so many others in India, where the flute could still be heard in the silken dusk of the evening.

They had gone there because of the work that Krishnabai and his wife Natasha were doing to build a village culture based on Gandhi's ideals of *swadeshi* (independence), *sarvodaya* (the welfare of all) and *shramdan* (community gifts of labour). While most of India was becoming noisier and more commercial, Sundareya remained a haven of beauty and simplicity, where the commitment to culture and community overcame the caste hostilities and religious bigotry of other places. Even the local Maoist guerrillas left Sundareya in peace out of respect for Krishnabai, and the work that he was doing to bring fulfillment and sustainability to all.

One year turned into ten, and when the Indian government granted them citizenship, Kerry and Lars knew they would stay forever. Kerry taught weaving, spinning and computer studies in the solar-powered village school, while Lars worked on the land with the other villagers, building the soil, planting trees and harvesting organic fruits and vegetables for sale in the markets of Patna and Bhagalpur.

The larger region of Orissa and southern Bihar was going through a terrible time, fuelled by an onslaught of World Bank-funded coal mines and chemical plants that polluted the air and water. At first, Kerry saw this as a challenge which made their efforts at Sundareya all the more important, but around the time when the Bengal tiger was declared extinct, in 2009, she began to notice some changes among the monkeys who liked to cavort in the trees above the temple to Kali. The juveniles were sporting strange, distorted genitals that produced no babies, however much they mated. Then Krishnabai and Natasha's daughter gave birth to a baby with a similarly misshapen sex organ, and three more followed in the local villages, including her own child. No one knew what was causing it, and the chemical companies denied any involvement, but when Kerry came across the article in *New Scientist* called "The End of Sex," it made the hairs rise on the back of her neck.

The writer showed how all around the world, male sperm counts were falling past the point of infertility. This was being caused, it seemed, by hormone-mimicking chemicals called phthalates which were leaching into our bodies from everyday things such as plastics, shampoos, drinking water and various foods. The article explained how certain combinations of the chemicals caused genital abnormalities and infertility in rats which drank water polluted with pesticides and phthalates. *Just like my baby* were the words that shot through Kerry's mind — and within seconds, she was vomiting on the earthen floor of their cottage.

In those few moments, Kerry's belief that they could turn this crazy, polluted world into a sustainable paradise vanished. All that was left was a black gory hole, as she stared into the remnants of what had been her faith. With the blinders off, all sorts of things fell into place. The frogs, which had vanished from the fields and farms all over India around the turn of the century, victims of the sun's UV rays that had burned their way into their floating spawn, destroying the DNA. The super-aggressive weeds, which had first appeared as escapees from the fields of genetically modified rice that the local farmers were growing. The harsh summer sun, which cut the skin and did funny things to the organic seedlings Lars tried to raise.

Kerry had thought they could tolerate the pollution from the open-pit coal mines, which blackened and toxified the local rivers, slowly killing the animals, plants and people who lived downstream. She had believed that, in time, their protests would force the World Bank and the G-9 supernations to stop their rapacious lending policies, based on the system of carbon credits which encouraged India to expand its output of fossil fuels, financed by the rich countries of the world. One day, she believed, the chemical companies would be forced to clean up their act, the coal mines would be replaced by windfarms and solar arrays, and the climate change that was pushing summer temperatures to a killing 48° C would stabilize.

But seen through the specter of her child's poor, twisted sex organ, a different, more ominous picture emerged. The world was not healing, as they hoped it would. It was growing sicker by the day — and to Kerry, it no longer seemed like the kind of sickness from which it would recover. The tigers were gone forever, except for the few unhappy creatures which paced the world's zoos. All over the world, temperatures were rising, wilderness lands were being trampled down and wild creatures were becoming extinct. This didn't feel like sickness: this felt more like death. If her baby and the millions being born with similar deformities couldn't reproduce, there would be no more children.

When Kerry was able to finish reading the article, she learned that the author of "The End of Sex" made the same prediction. If the trend continued, the world's population would plunge from 6.8 billion to two billion within four generations. Many species of mammal and reptile would be similarly affected. With so many fewer humans around to mess up the world, the climate might gain the breathing space it needed to stabilize, and the forests might eventually recover, but the tigers, the mountain gorillas, the orangutans, the thousands of other species — they would all be gone forever.

Lars believed in the Hindu philosophy, which said that life was a cycle of sorrow from which the wise person sought to escape by achieving spiritual enlightenment, leaving forever the woeful wheel of reincarnation. Kerry had never accepted that. She used to believe that underneath its many tragedies, life was still beautiful, and that spiritually, "all would be well." As soon as we learned to co-operate and live sustainably, she used to argue, Earth would be well too.

But that was before she knew what she knew today. Maybe in a thousand years, Kerry thought, Earth would recover, and a wounded Gaia would continue her journey into the future, older but wiser for her hurts. But oh, Kerry felt with every tired cell in her body, oh, how it hurt.

Notes

For information about phthalates and genetic abnormalities, see *Our Stolen Future: Are We Threatening Our Fertility, Intelligence and Survival?* by Theo Colborn, Dianne Dumanoski and John Myers (Dutton, 1996). For data on the falling male sperm count, see "Some of our Sperm are Missing" in the *New Scientist*, 26 August 1995. A good way to keep up-to-date is to subscribe to *Rachel's Environment and Health Weekly* ($25 US per year from the Environmental Research Foundation, PO Box 5036, Annapolis, Maryland, 21403-7036, USA; erf@rachel.clark.net).

The frogs are disappearing all over the world. The jury is still out on the cause, but UV rays are the leading suspect. The Bengal tigers of India are extremely endangered, as are the mountain gorillas and the orangutans. The pollen from genetically modified corn has been found to kill the Monarch butterfly; superweeds are bound to be Nature's response to genetically modified plants designed to resist huge quantities of herbicide.

The Indian state of Orissa is being devastated by World Bank-financed coal mining projects, led by the G-7 nations. A 1998 report by the Institute for Policy Studies, *Destroying Orissa*, explains how after the 1992 Rio Earth Summit, when the poor countries in the South were given time to "develop their economies" before reducing their greenhouse gas emissions, the rich countries responded by using the World Bank to funnel massive quantities of capital into coal mining and coal-fired power plants in places like Orissa. It describes how the massive exploitation of coal and other minerals has unleashed a torrent of destruction. Rivers carry toxic effluent through villages where people rely on the blackened waters for bathing, drinking and washing their clothes. The black water of the Nandira, once a life-sustaining river, is slowly poisoning and killing people, animals, fish and plants as far away as fifty miles downstream. Agricultural productivity has dropped for farmers dependent on its water; fishing communities have been wiped out. The incidence of cancer, bronchitis and skin diseases are all soaring. See *The World Bank's Juggernaut: The Coal-Fired Industrial Colonization of the Indian State of Orissa and The G-7, the World Bank, and Climate Change*, $7 each from Institute for Policy Studies, 733 – 15th Street NW, Suite 1020, Washington, DC 20005, USA; **www.ips-dc.org**.

Antarctica's Farewell

New Ross Bay, Antarctica
February 2050

Thor Magnusson paddled his kayak slowly across the vast New Ross Bay, this ocean of emptiness that had not existed ten years before. To the south, the towering TransAntarctic Mountains rose steeply from the ocean's edge, discharging their multi-million-year-old ice down countless glaciers, feeding the ever-rising sea.

As a geologist, he should have seen it coming. His father had warned Thor and his brother that theirs would be a generation fated to witness global catastrophe on an unprecedented scale unless they slowed global warming and halted humanity's "parade of fools," as he termed it. Thor had listened, and while at school he had even written letters to the world's leaders, urging protection for the world's tigers. Once out of college, however, his new job and his marriage had relegated his father's words to the status of "some day." He had a career to develop and a son to support. Why should he not enjoy one of those ultramarine, gas-electric sports utility vehicles, like the rest of his geologist colleagues? They were, after all, supposed to be so environmentally friendly, so fuel efficient.

Today, in the silence of this awful, majestic place, all of that seemed like another life. His wife Marguerite was gone, drowned in a flash flood while holidaying in Kenya. The community where they had lived so happily among his fellow geologists near Modesto, California, was gone, abandoned under the water that had come pouring up the Central Valley. And now his precious son Bjørn was lost, assumed drowned, while attempting to kayak from Hammerfest in Norway's far north to the North Pole, endeavoring to be the first human ever to cross the Arctic Ocean alone in a human-powered boat.

If Thor were to kayak due north from New Ross Bay, following the 170th line of longitude, he would not encounter a single piece of land before he reached the place where Bjørn's spirit must now be wandering. What was it about the Norwegians, he wondered, that gave them such an obsession with being the first, the best, the fastest? Maybe it was living so close to Sweden. Or maybe they shared their folly with all humanity. They were certainly sharing the grief that accompanied the folly.

Thor had been so sure Antarctica would never change. Among his professional geologist colleagues, he was of the "stabilist" persuasion, who believed that the Antarctic continent had been unchanged for eight million years, and was among the most stable geological features on the planet. If only he had been less proud, and more able to listen to the warnings from his colleagues in the "dynamist" camp, who insisted that Antarctica had collapsed before, and could collapse again.

It was stupid, he realized with painful sadness, that professional scientists should be so attached to their theories. If he had only understood, perhaps he could have helped the dynamists in their vain attempts to warn the world. If only he had been less concerned with trivial things like the way he dressed. If only he had paused to remember his father's warnings, perhaps he could have done something to stop this incomprehensible tragedy.

The grandeur of the looming mountains was amplified by the ice-streams that poured down from the glaciers into the sea. Ten kilometers a year did not seem a particularly impressive speed at which to drown the world. Yet there they were, those tongues of ice moving slowly northwards into the ocean, inundating the civilized world at ten kilometers a year, twenty-seven meters a day. All for a hundred years of fun and fast living, burning a hundred millions years of stored solar energy — fossil-fuels.

And now, the 20,000-year hangover. This was the price that Earth would pay for its hundred years of folly. The coastal civilizations, the farmlands, the thousand-year-old temples and palaces, all gone, drowned, abandoned to the waters. The ocean islands, the Maldives, the Polynesian paradises, vanished as if they had never existed. The 70 million refugees struggling for comfort in impoverished camps, half-starved because so much of the world's farmland had been lost to the ocean. The remaining farmlands ravaged by annual grassland fires. The scourges of malaria and yellow fever eating their way through healthy Italians, Germans and Canadians, whose bodies had never developed genetic immunity to these tropical diseases. The nuclear reactors whose defenses had not been sufficiently watertight, that had released their burden of radioactivity into the world's oceans. There were no words sufficient to describe the scale of what had happened.

As Norwegians, Thor and his friends had done their share of enjoying the good life. For as long as Thor could remember, every Norwegian had been guaranteed wealth and prosperity from the cradle to the grave, thanks to the revenues that successive Norwegian governments had squirreled away from North Sea oil. Norwegians had enjoyed comfortable oil-heated homes, comfortable cars, and comfortable holidays in comfortable places, reached by comfortable oil-devouring airplanes that poured their carbon dioxide and nitrous oxide into the heart of the uncomfortable upper atmosphere.

But while Thor and his stabilist friends had been enjoying themselves kayaking along the world's most beautiful coastlines, his dynamist colleagues had been frantically touring the world, warning whoever would listen about this terrible thing that was about to happen unless they woke up and took the climate-change crisis seriously. "Jeremiahs," Thor's friends had called them, facetiously.

Today, it was all too late. Too late for Thor, too late for Marguerite, too late for the millions who had lost their homes, their families, their ancestral homelands. If only, Thor thought soberly, as he paddled closer to the gigantic cliffs. If only we had heeded the warnings instead of worshipping the God of Oil so fervently, delivering tax-breaks and subsidies to the oil companies like some kind of tribute to a heathen deity. If only we had heeded the wisdom of the Dutch and the Danes, with their windmills and solar roofs. If only we had listened to the thousand young Dutch boys and girls who had cycled around the globe in a desperate effort to make the world wake up and embrace the solar revolution, before it was too late. If only. Their homeland was gone now, lost forever under twenty feet of ocean.

The solar and wind technologies, the hydrogen fuel cells, the triple-glazed, energy-saving windows had all been ready. Nothing had prevented the world from making the switch, apart from comfort, laziness and greed — and those lavish banquets that the oil companies laid on at the stabilists' annual conventions. How many such banquets would Thor now reject, if he had known the price? Talk about the devil's bargain. All around the world, there was such confusion, turmoil and suffering. His father's poor spirit must be reeling in shock in whichever district of heaven good Norwegians went to.

It was the tundra that had been their final undoing. As the Arctic temperatures warmed, the frozen tundra began to melt, releasing vast quantities of methane into an atmosphere already overburdened with greenhouse gases. The global treaties to reduce emissions had never worked; their targets had always been too vague, their loopholes too many. The oil companies had made their promises, but they were too little, too late, and they were reluctant to close down their oil production and move entirely to renewable energy until the disaster was already in progress. It had all been a massive joke, a trick they had played on humanity.

As far back as the year 2000, Thor recalled, the dynamists had been warning that we needed to rid ourselves of half our fossil fuel consumption by 2025, and the rest by 2050, if we were to have a chance to stabilize the planet's steadily warming climate. We knew that the glaciers were melting, the oceans were warming, the krill were disappearing. Why did we not see it as a warning when the blue whales became extinct, starved to death for the lack of krill? With the shelf-ice and its coating of algae gone, the krill could no longer feed, and without the krill, the whales could not survive. A hundred million years of existence, snapped out in the passing of a family van. Hence the Greenpeace slogan, *Drive a Car, Starve a Whale*. How could we been such useless stewards, such hopeless guardians of the Earth?

It had been the same with the salmon. In Norway, of all places, they should have seen that as a sign. The salmon were biologically unable to survive in waters warmer than 7° Celsius, and as the oceans warmed, the salmon moved further and further north, until they could no longer migrate home to spawn in the rivers of their birth.

With the Earth's temperature as warm as it had been in the Pliocene Era, the bulk of the West Antarctic's and much of Greenland's ice had gone, and sea levels around the world had risen by twenty feet — not the meager three feet the stabilists said would occur over a period of a hundred years. Now it was the East Antarctic Ice Sheet directing its mountains of ice toward the ocean. Ten thousand feet high, the ice sheet poured through the towering Trans-Antarctic Mountains to the ocean. If all of that ice were to be released, the world's sea levels would rise by another forty feet. If only the tears of the grieving millions could undo this awful tragedy, instead of making it worse.

So what now? What use were anger, grief, or shame to undo this liquid holocaust that was entombing so much of the civilized world in a catacomb of water? The ocean had already claimed so many millions. It would be so easy to end it all, Thor thought. Take off the life-jacket, unzip the thermal bodysuit and slip into the sea. It would all be over by the time his mother-ship realized something was wrong.

But that would be too easy. The least that he owed the millions who had lost their lives in the storms and famines was to live the rest of his life in honest shame and regret — that when he could have acted, he did so little; and when he could have remembered, he forgot.

Notes

The West Antarctic Ice Sheet is already breaking up, as global temperatures rise. If the whole ice-sheet collapsed, sea levels would rise by twenty feet. This is a realistic portrayal of what could happen if we fail to stop using fossil fuels.

Most of the West Antarctic Ice Sheet is less than 600,000 years old. 120,000 years ago, when the planet enjoyed a climate and sea level similar to today's, there was a "Madhouse Century" when sea levels rose by twenty feet around the world, then fell by fifty feet. The only possible explanation is that something caused the West Antarctic Ice Sheet to collapse, flooding the world with a twelve percent increase in water, which triggered a sudden drop in temperature and brought on an ice age that created new polar ice-fields, lowering the world's oceans as the ice formed (see *New Scientist* magazine, August 1995). The East Antarctic Ice Sheet is estimated to be between eleven and seventeen million years old.

Many thanks to Rhys Roth (Climate Solutions), Andy Caffrey (Climate Action NOW!) and Terence Hughes (Institute for Quaternary Studies, University of Maine) for their assistance with this story. For further information, see **www.pbs.org/wgbh/nova/warnings**.

The Economists' Celebration

Paris, France
December 2012

The whole room was swinging with the sensual rhythms of the gypsy violin as Bo Larssen and his fellow economists enjoyed a well-deserved evening of dancing, singing and jazz at Le Hot Club Grappelli, on the Rue de Rivoli in the heart of Paris. They were exultant.

What a triumph! On Monday, Bo had been the proud recipient of the Nobel Prize for Economic Sciences for his work in co-budgeting, awarded by King Carl Gustav in the grandeur of Stockholm's beautiful Concert Hall, with all of Sweden watching. On Tuesday he had addressed the European Union's Council of Ministers in Brussels, and yesterday he had been treated to a private lunch at one of Paris's top restaurants with Marcel Duceppe, the French Minister of Finance. All week long the European financial media had been chasing him for interviews.

The economists' good humor gave Le Hot Club that extra charge, bringing out the best in the musicians. Bo's wife, Dagmar, was sitting across from him, playing footsie with him under the table while he told his fellow economists about his lunch with Duceppe, laughing at how little the minister knew about the principles of integrative and disintegrative budgeting. Speaking in Swedish, they felt free to be outrageously rude, knowing that hardly anyone in France understood Swedish.

Bo and Dagmar were in their early forties, and brought a much appreciated glamor to the economists' social circle. After years of being the butt of such jokes as "Why did so-and-so become an economist? Because he lacked the charisma to become an accountant," or "Why did God make economists? To make weather-forecasters look exciting," it felt good to have done something so radical that they had become the envy of the academic crowd. Watching Dagmar flick her blond hair back while flirting with the lead violinist made up for all the years of Swedish philosophers sneering at them, saying (for the hundredth time), "An economist is a man who knows a hundred ways to make love, but doesn't know any women." Well, guess who was laughing now — and to rub it in, co-budgeting was grounded in the most exciting breakthrough in philosophy since Descartes announced the birth of dualism with his *Discourse on Method* and unceremoniously dumped integrative thinking into the Seine, almost 400 years ago.

To tell the truth, co-budgeting had not started with Bo Larssen's interest in integrative philosophy and syntropy theory. It had started with Bo's step-son, Tord, Dagmar's son by her first marriage. As teenagers, Dagmar and her first husband had been heavy drinkers, with the tragic result that their son Tord was born with fetal alcohol syndrome (alcohol poisoning of the fetus), though it was not diagnosed until he was six years old. When Tord was four, Dagmar divorced her husband, joined Alcoholics Anonymous, and then fell in love with Bo. Bo took an immediate liking to Tord, but sensed there was something seriously wrong, for while Tord was very affectionate, he was slow to learn, impulsive, and easily influenced by his friends, who used to enjoy getting him into trouble.

As an economist, Bo specialized in full (or social) cost accounting, the difficult art of measuring the hidden costs of things such as air pollution or inadequate childhood diet, and bringing them into the open. It had always frustrated him that for the lack of a relatively small expenditure at the beginning of a problem, there were often such enormous costs at the end. If only he could find a way to link the two ends, and allow the principles of investment and return to work in the social realm, the same way that they did in the business realm.

Tord's difficulties fuelled Bo's frustration. Digging into the research on fetal alcohol syndrome, he discovered that as many as twenty percent of the occupants of Europe's prisons were believed to be victims of the syndrome, costing the taxpayers enormous sums of money every year to pay for the crime, the legal costs, the time in prison and the subsequent rehabilitation. If as little as one percent of these costs could be spent on pre-natal education and alcohol counseling, many of the later expenditures could be avoided, generating potentially massive returns. If only he could demonstrate the budgetary connections in such a way that it would entice investors to finance the front-end expenditures. The disintegrative nature of traditional budgeting lay at the root of the problem, breaking the deeper connections.

Bo was struggling with the problem in 2006 when he, Dagmar and Tord took a holiday in Tuscany. Bo took some reading to catch up on, including the bestseller *Syntropy* by Iqbal Kharoun and Elizabeth Mitchell, which was the talk of the world. Syntropy was the newly discovered tendency of all consciousness to seek organization and integration, the mirror image of entropy, which was the tendency of matter and energy to become disorganized. It was syntropy that provided evolution's fuel as it groped its way towards greater consciousness and wholeness. It was syntropy that inspired the eternal tango between hope and defeat, spiritual drive and material decay. By placing consciousness firmly at the heart of all that exists, Kharoun and Mitchell re-integrated consciousness into the heart of reality, not just in physics and the life sciences, but within the human spirit.

Bo was enthralled. This tension between syntropy and entropy was the very same tension he was struggling with in his budgetary problems. Surely, he thought, as he gazed on Tuscany's peaceful villas and distant hills, disintegrative budgeting was just another reflection of social entropy. What was needed, he realized with a flash, was syntropic budgeting, integrative budgeting — budgeting which would start from the premise that all things were connected and would go on to construct an entire assemblage of connections, linking the previously isolated departments. All over the world, governments put "law and order" in one department and "social welfare" in another; "environmental protection" in one department and "health" in another, when their natural state was connection, not separation. Looking up at the brilliant blue of the Italian summer sky, Bo knew that it could be done, and that he would be the one to do it.

Back amidst the falling leaves of Stockholm's autumn, he immersed himself in the world of chaos theory, meta-organizational principles, and integrational software programs. To anyone outside the enclosed world of the university economics department, it would have appeared incomprehensible, but as Bo worked, he kept a photo of Tord on his desk to remind him that he was working both for Tord and for the millions of Tords all over the world, wherever the inefficiencies of disintegrative budgeting undermined the principles of social and ecological wholeness.

In the spring of 2008 he presented his work to the Swedish Ministry of Finance, and that fall the government set up a pilot project linking the budget for crime and prisons to the budget for youth and community development. Swedish studies indicated that for every krona invested in community development and youth projects, seven krona could be saved in prison and legal costs. By linking the budgets through an integrative loop, an expenditure in one department could be turned into a saving in the other, and an investment could be made to generate a return. Once the process was in place, the government invited the public to invest $100 million in social bonds, with the promise of a good long-term return on their investment, potentially as high as 700 percent over twenty years, reflecting the sevenfold nature of the losses that occurred through disintegrative budgeting. Suddenly the sleepy world of budgetary finance was awake with incoming e-mails, and long before the investments had a chance to render their returns, people were paying attention.

Over the next three years the principles of co-budgeting were extended to other departments. In addition to social bonds, Swedish investors were able to purchase health bonds, family bonds and ecological bonds, the money from which was used to finance investments in a range of projects designed to heal a certain aspect of society. For a relatively small investment in making the homes of elderly people safer against falls, for instance, investors could enjoy a 300 percent return on the budget savings from avoided accidents and their associated medical costs.

Sitting that night with his wife and friends in Le Hot Club Grappelli, Bo knew that even while they celebrated, the social bonds he and Dagmar had purchased were paying for the additional help that Tord needed in school, to protect him from his fetal alcohol impulsiveness. Across the world, in the watersheds of Washington and British Columbia, ecological bonds were financing the restoration of salmon stocks, while in Alabama and Texas, family bonds were being used to finance premarital relationship courses for young couples, to increase their chance of enjoying stable, successful marriages. He felt proud that his work was being recognized around the world. The night was young, and the music was good. He had worked hard to earn this. "Hej — Dagmar, Jan, Kerstin. Hej — Eric! Skol! Here's to all those boring Swedish philosophers!" And they laughed together, raising their glasses of ice-cocktail guava juice.

Notes

I have coined the word "co-budgeting," but I do not know of any country where the idea is being practiced yet. It is widely accepted that a dollar spent on programs for youth at risk saves $7 in prison and legal costs, and that's not counting the emotional and personal costs to the teenagers and their families, or the victims of their crimes. Similarly, a dollar spent on measures that help to prevent older people from falling saves $11 on medical bills. Once we start thinking in terms of wholeness, there are many synergies and positive mechanisms which can work to the benefit of humans, nature and the planet.

Nurjahan's Story

I don't understand why anybody should be poor on this planet.
Muhammad Yunus, 1997

Sarishpur, Bangladesh
April 2013

I was born in 1971, the year Bangladesh fought its way to independence from Pakistan and became a nation. My name, Nurjahan, means "the light of the world."

I never knew my real parents. I have been told that my grandfather was a wealthy peasant farmer who owned six acres, who had five sons and a daughter. Each time one of his sons married, he sold a piece of land to pay for the wedding. When his daughter married, he sold more land to provide her with a dowry. By the time of his death he owned one acre, which was divided between his five sons.

My father, Abu, was his fifth son. When Abu married my mother, she was often sick, so Abu had to sell part of his acre to buy medicines. He sold more of it to the local moneylender to repay a family debt, and by the time I was born, there was none left. Then came the civil war, and in the confusion of it all, my parents fled the village, leaving me with a neighbor. I was three months old.

I think of Komla as my mother. She and her husband Shafiqal were landless labourers who worked in the fields for a pittance with two children of their own. During the famine of 1974, when the rice was being hoarded by the merchants and sold for fifty times its normal price, they were forced to gather wild greens and roots to keep us alive. One of my earliest memories is of searching in the dirt outside the merchants' houses, looking for grains that might have fallen from their sacks. Komla's youngest child died during the famine.

We lived all together in the poorest of shacks. Our floor was packed mud; the roof was made from sagging straw that would collapse every monsoon so that the rain came in and soaked everything; the walls were made from a few dried palm leaves, hung on bamboo poles. We had no furniture. We slept together on burlap bags laid on the floor. In the winter, Komla stuffed straw into a bag to cover us against the cold. We were always hungry. Sometimes Shafiqal would lose a job because he was too weak to do the work, for lack of food.

When I was twelve, they married me off to a rickshaw driver from Bajitpur, the nearby town, in exchange for my dowry — a new sari and a small gift of money. It was horrible. My husband — I have vowed never to speak his name again — would come home drunk every night and beat me, then force me to lie with him. Then he started bringing other women home. They would shout at me and treat me like a servant, expecting me to cook for them while they had sex with my husband on the other side of a screen. I never knew which was worse, lying with him myself, or listening while he lay with these other women.

After a year, when I was two months pregnant, one of his women became very angry and demanded that he throw me out. I sat outside the door for three days, crying and asking to be let back in, but he just came out and kicked me. None of the neighbors helped. I didn't come from their families, so they owed me nothing. In the end, I picked myself up and walked the seven miles back to Sarishpur, where Komla and Shafiqal took me in and let me stay while I raised my son, Siddique. I was thirteen years old. Komla and her husband have always been kind, no matter how little they had. Sometimes when there was no money, Komla would go for days without food, chewing betel nuts to dull the stomach pains, while feeding us any scraps of food she could find.

They were kind to me three years later, too, when I fell in love with a boy from a nearby village. I am still ashamed of myself. I must have encouraged him, because one day when we were walking by the rice paddies, I softened to his advances. Two months later, I became pregnant again. I know it was wrong. Other families would have thrown me out. But

Shafiqal simply said, "If Allah wishes you to have his child, you will have his child."

My boyfriend's family were furious, and we were forbidden to see each other. They called me a prostitute, a fallen woman — all sorts of terrible things. If we had lived in Pakistan, they would probably have given me a hundred lashes and then stoned me to death — or poured cooking oil over me and set me on fire.

That was the darkest time of my life. There were times when I cried all day and all night, wishing that I had never been born. Siddique was three and always crying from hunger. When there was nothing to eat, I would walk the seven miles into Bajitpur with Siddique on my hip and spend the day begging outside the bus station. I had to sit on the roadside, competing with the lepers, the men with no legs who got around on little wooden trays on wheels, and children whose limbs had been deliberately broken by their parents to make them better beggars. I was terribly ashamed. Sometimes a man offered to take me somewhere in a taxi. Most of the time I refused, but when we were really hungry, I would leave Siddique with another beggar woman and go with them. It was horrible, but I had to feed Siddique. I had to live. Luckily, Komla never found out that I was doing this. Sharifa, my daughter, must have wanted to be born very much. If she hadn't, I'm sure I would have had a miscarriage. Allah must have loved her and wanted her to live.

Today, Siddique wears a smart suit and drives a fast yellow car. He looks very important with his well-groomed hair and his cellular telephone. He is a regional director with Grameen Shakti (Grameen Power), where he advises farmers how to set up solar and windpower co-operatives. He has even been to America.

My daughter Sharifa is a teacher here in Sarishpur and is studying for a distance-learning degree in education from the Open University, in England. She has a good husband and two daughters, who live with Komla and myself in our new house, with our garden and our solarvoltaic roof. Shafiqal died seven years ago. This week Sharifa is away in Dhaka, where she is speaking at an international conference on poverty and family planning. We own six acres of land, where we grow rice, and we own four pigs, three goats, five cows, a hundred chickens and a share in a fishpond. We live in a clean, well-built house, and I pay thirty taka a year into a community health plan. I contribute to a mutual fund for my retirement for when I am too old to work, and Komla does the same. We cook with the biogas that our pigs produce, and we harvest our own fruit and vegetables, which we have learnt to grow organically, using compost instead of expensive chemicals. We are part owners in a farmers' windpower co-operative, and the roof of our house is covered in solar shingles, which give us the power we need for lighting, a radio, and the computer Siddique gave me to keep in touch with him by video-mail. I sit on the advisory committee of the Sarishpur Grameen Bank and am chairwoman of the Reforestation Co-operative. Every day, when I arise before dawn, I give thanks to Allah for the miracles he has given us, and I give thanks to Muhammad Yunus, who made it all possible.

• • •

I still ask myself — how did this happen? It started on a day in February 1991, when a woman from the Grameen Bank came to Sarishpur looking for women to form a lending circle. She only wanted the very poorest women, who would never receive a loan from a regular bank.

I was twenty years old and had never been near a bank. When Komla and her husband needed money, they went to a moneylender. They couldn't go to a bank, because they had no land to use as collateral for a loan. The moneylenders charged ten percent per day. If you borrowed fifty taka, you had to repay fifty-five taka tomorrow. That was how the moneylenders grew rich — and how the rest of us grew so poor. They didn't call it interest, because Muslim law doesn't allow that, but they still did it. That's a kind of prostitution, too.

Komla was very suspicious about the new bank. She didn't want me going to the meeting, but I was interested. What kind of people wanted to help a woman like me? There were thirty of us at the first meeting. By the time we finished, I had agreed to join a circle with four other women from the village. We had to decide which two of us would receive the first loans, and what we were going to use them for. The Grameen Bank didn't require any collateral, and they didn't require our husbands or fathers to sign the loans for us, but if the first two did not repay their loans, the rest of our group would not be able to borrow. We were suddenly together, and we had to help each other. As women, we knew what our troubles were. We never thought to waste the money, or spend it on stupid things. The interest was just twenty percent a year, and we had to start repaying the loan within two weeks.

I decided to borrow 200 taka to buy three chickens, repaying the loan by selling the eggs. The chickens did fine, and six months later I was able to apply for a second loan, which I used to buy a very small portion of land and a goat. By milking the goat every morning and evening, I was able to repay this loan too, so then I applied for a third loan to buy a cow. That's how it started. By the time I had my third loan, Komla had joined a circle too. She received her first loan to buy a sewing machine, which she used to do clothing repairs. One of the women in my circle used her loan to fatten her cow, while another used it to get her rice husked.

One of the things we had to do if we wanted to receive a loan was think about the Grameen Bank's "16 Decisions," and take an oral exam to show that we understood them. The woman from the bank said they were very important and would help us build better lives. The one that caused the most discussion was "We shall not take any dowry at the time of marriage of our sons, and we shall not give any dowry at the time of marriage of our daughters." This meant breaking with a very powerful tradition. The thought that I might not have to find a dowry for Sharifa was very liberating. Many mothers cursed the day they gave birth to a daughter, and often wished her dead, even to her face. We lived with the daily knowledge that when our daughters married, we would have to sell whatever we had and go to the moneylender to pay for their dowries. If we did not, our daughters would not be able to find good husbands. If we took this pledge, however, our daughters could find themselves good husbands by marrying sons from families which had also taken the pledge.

We also had to decide that we wanted to change our lives; that we wanted to live in a well-built house; that we wanted to send our children to school so that they could become educated; that we wanted to ensure a healthy environment around us; that we wanted to grow trees; that we would grow vegetables all year round, eat plenty of them, and sell the surplus.

I was lucky — I had no husband to tell me I couldn't do these things. Some of the women had a terrible time persuading their husbands to let them continue. They said it was a Christian plot or a Western scheme to destroy the Muslim faith. As soon as they started bringing cows and banana seedlings home, however, their husbands began to change.

At the time when the Grameen Bank came to Sarishpur in 1991, it was already established in 25,000 villages in Bangladesh, providing three million loans a year to very poor women like myself. The bank started in the mind of Muhammad Yunus, an economics professor from Chittagong who was frustrated with the dull economic theories he and his colleagues were teaching while people were starving to death in the nearby villages. He started by lending his own personal money to very poor women, observing how they would use it to improve their lives and then repay him. In the end, he persuaded the government to let him set up a bank — but one that was different from any other bank in the world.

The lending program grew and grew, and people began to copy it in other countries. An English author wrote that "the Grameen Bank is probably the single most important social invention of the twentieth century: it demonstrates the power and vitality of community economic development with extraordinary success." Others have written petitions, nominating Muhammad Yunus for the Nobel Prize for Peace. By the time I was thirty, if you counted all the micro-credit programs inspired by Grameen, this unique kind of peer-group circle lending was reaching sixty million of the world's poorest families.

I still find it strange to use big words like "micro-credit." I never went to school, and I never learned to read or write as a child. It was only after I received my third loan that the Grameen committee encouraged me to join a literacy class and learn to read. It took me a year, but then it was as if a candle had been lit inside my head. Someone gave me a book of poems by the Bengali poet Rabindranath Tagore, and I loved them so much that I learned them by heart, getting up early each morning to read before the day started. I began to remember how many cruel words had been spoken to me and women like myself, who never had the chance to go to school. We were treated like dirt. Nobody had any respect for us. So I started teaching other women to read. Everyone should have this excitement, I thought, to travel on flights of imagination through the poetry of the printed word.

When I was twenty-five, the local Grameen committee turned its attention to the problems of the land. In Sarishpur, as in so many Bangladeshi villages, the land is scattered among many small landholders, making it difficult to irrigate. There was no shortage of water. Bangladesh is full of water from the three huge rivers that flow through it, but it takes co-operation to set up an irrigation system. The Grameen Bank set up an organization called the Grameen Agricultural Foundation (GAF), which showed us how by pooling our land into a fifty-acre "Primary Farm," we could irrigate it with a single deep tubewell. We still own our own land, but the GAF brings us together. It helps us to co-operate.

The GAF financed the well and the irrigation system, and we paid for it by selling a share of our crop — no money was needed. I had one acre of land by then, and I soon discovered that my irrigated field was producing twice as much as before. The GAF helped me to buy fertilizer, seeds and farm equipment. Before, I often had to sell my crop as soon as I had finished harvesting, often at a terrible price. GAF helped me to store the rice, and then trucked it to Dhaka for me, where I got a much better price.

Later, I got together with my immediate neighbors to create a shared fishpond. I took out a loan to buy another two acres, and I was able to pay to send Siddique and Sharifa to the village school. This was a very exciting time. My income was increasing every year, and the future was looking good.

In the late 1990s, the Grameen Bank started moving into all sorts of new areas. None of the villages in our region had power, and it would be years before electrification arrived, so Grameen Shakti was born. Using the same system of lending, women were encouraged to become solar and biogas dealers. Later, we set up our windpower co-operative, starting with a Vestas wind turbine from Denmark to meet the needs of the village.

At the same time, the Grameen Phone company and Grameen Cybernet were set up. I didn't think I knew anyone outside the village to call, but once the cellular phone was in place, run by a woman as a small business, I started calling the GAF to discuss harvesting details and market prices. It was Siddique who showed me how to use the Internet. They had one at the school, powered by solar energy from the school's rooftop. When Siddique showed me the messages he was receiving in English from a school in America, I could hardly believe it. I had never traveled more than seven miles from Sarishpur. Suddenly, the world had become a much bigger place.

Since 2000, the changes we have seen in Sarishpur have been amazing. Many of us women who used to struggle in poverty have steady, reliable incomes. Komla and I took out a loan to build ourselves a new house, which Siddique fitted with a solar shingles roof and a biogas plant for cooking. We built ourselves a garden and planted fruit trees. Grandmother Komla joined Grameen Check, working at home as a hand-weaver to produce Bangladesh's traditional cotton check fabric, that is exported around the world.

Now everyone in our family is working. Sharifa's husband and I work in the fields, planting, weeding and harvesting the rice. Komla is at home, weaving, and Sharifa teaches at the village school, where the children learn about micro-enterprise by running their own businesses. The Grameen Bank has even set up a daycare center, where Sharifa's children play while we're working. At the end of the day, we eat well.

One of the good things about the Grameen Bank is that women who join the lending circles have fewer children. Sharifa has become very involved in family planning, and is working to make sure that every woman in the village has the information and the contraceptive supplies to limit her family to one or two children. The women in the lending circles also suffer less violence from their husbands, and have fewer divorces. It used to be that very few women could read or write. Today, almost everyone can. The ponds and rice paddies are alive with fish, and the village is full of coconut, mango and jackfruit trees. Many of the houses have garden trellises covered with climbing squash and beans, which taste a lot better than the wild greens, roots and grasshoppers we used to eat when I was a child. It is quite unusual today for children to suffer from night blindness caused by a vitamin A deficiency, because they are not getting enough to eat.

We have been planting thousands of trees to stabilize the river banks and absorb some of the surplus carbon dioxide that is pouring out of the world's chimneys and cars. Here in Bangladesh, we face a terrible threat from flooding. Every year, the monsoon rains seem to get heavier and the typhoons that surge in from the Bay of Bengal get stronger, destroying more villages and drowning more people. Sarishpur is inland, away from the worst of the weather, but along with most of Bangladesh, we are only a few feet above sea level. If the world's sea level rises by as much as some people are predicting, our whole village will drown. It will be the end of us, and everything we have been struggling to achieve. We will have to flee and become refugees in someone else's village, like the families that have been arriving in Sarishpur from the south, having to start all over again from nothing.

When we were living in poverty, global warming seemed very unfair. It was like a plot by the world's richest countries to undermine the poorest countries. Why should we have to suffer because they lived such wasteful lives? As we started to grow more prosperous, however, the same thing began to happen here. The wealthy landowners started to buy jeeps and four-wheel-drive trucks and seduced the young men into wanting to drive. With solar energy in the village, people were buying televisions, where they saw movies full of violence, sex and fast cars. The rich people took it as their right to drive their cars wherever they wanted, causing huge fights and arguments. Even my own son loved to borrow a friend's car and drive around the village at top speed, chasing the chickens and frightening everyone.

135

We were not alone with this problem. It was happening throughout Bangladesh, wherever the Grameen Bank was bringing prosperity to the villages. We wanted progress, but we liked the old traditional ways, where we walked around on foot without fear of being killed by a car. Cars are for the city, where everyone drives like a maniac, not for a place like Sarishpur, where everyone knows each other by name.

The Grameen Bank's solution was threefold. Firstly, they encouraged us to stick to the decision we had made about protecting the environment, so we closed off the village center to motorized vehicles. This was very controversial, since the families who own the cars are also the wealthiest and most powerful. There were many more of us who do not own a car, however, and after a big argument, we won.

Secondly, they established a new organization called Grameen Transport, and gave us loans to buy bicycles and bicycle trailers. For the longer trips, they helped us establish the Sarishpur car-share co-operative, which gives us shared ownership of a truck, a minibus and three electrically-assisted bicycle-trailers. Grameen Shakti and Grameen Transport have just signed a partnership with Sanyota, the Japanese solar-automobile conglomerate, and we are going to build ten new Vestas wind turbines on our land, using the energy to manufacture hydrogen for the hydrogen-fuelled vehicles that Sanyota is manufacturing for developing countries. We'll use some of the fuel in our own vehicles, and sell the rest to Sanyota for use in Dhaka, where there is such terrible air pollution. The hydrogen vehicles produce no greenhouse gases and give off only water as a waste product, so it is a very good arrangement that will bring us extra income.

On one level, I have never been happier. We no longer live in poverty. We own six acres of land, as my grandfather used to do. I have two very happy and successful children, and two granddaughters. I have come a long way since the days of begging in the dirt of Bajitpur. Today I wear a clean sari, and carry a gold pin in my nose. But I also see lots of troubling signs. The television is encouraging people to waste their money on all sorts of unnecessary things, and the Internet allows our children to see terrible videos of real sex and naked bodies, which I find very shocking. When I did it, I knew it was wrong, but we had to survive. Today, the young men seem to think they have a right to make love to the girls before they are married.

I am also troubled because the big global corporations have seen how successful the Grameen Bank has become and are trying to set up all sorts of partnerships with Grameen. Some have been good, like the ones with Sanyota and Vestas, but others have not. It started with Mongrando, in the 1990s. They tried to persuade Grameen to partner with them to buy their genetically modified seeds. We would have had to buy new seeds from Mongrando every year and to spray their chemical pesticides on our rice. Luckily there was a worldwide protest by people who knew about Mongrando's dirty tricks, and they persuaded Muhammad Yunus to scrap the deal.

Next it was MacDonuts, who wanted a Grameen franchise to set up a fast food restaurant in every village. We had to fight them off, too. Then it was Global Telus, who tried to sell us the very same phone cards that had almost caused a war in France. The cards were invented in Italy and featured a fully clothed woman who slowly undressed each time you used one of the units on the card, until she was completely naked. The Italians thought nothing of it, but the Arab community in France was outraged, especially because one of the women on the cards had been given a darker skin and looked like a famous Egyptian singer. Someone must have forgotten to tell the Italian company that Bangladesh was a Muslim country, where the sight of the female body is totally taboo. The Grameen Bank has always tried to be totally transparent, and they keep us informed by a weekly newsletter that we get through the village e-mail. Bangladesh is notoriously full of corruption, but by being open, we have avoided the disease. It was only because of the Grameen Bank's openness that we learned about the MacDonuts and Global Telus proposals, and were able to send messages back, asking to stop them. We did the same when Mongrando came back with another proposal, five years later. This time, they were proposing to finance improvements to all of our wells and irrigation systems, in exchange for part ownership. We told them "NO!" It looks as if they are trying to take over all of the world's food and water, the way they are behaving.

Sharifa studies a lot, as well as teaching and going to big conferences. She tells me that the micro-lending that has transformed our lives here in Sarishpur is being used all over the world to lift people out of poverty. They want to abolish poverty so that it becomes something you learn about in museums, not in real life, she says. She says micro-lending is reaching 170 million of the world's poorest families, or 850 million people, and that by the year 2025 they hope to reach all of the world's poorest people.

She says that half the people who receive loans through lending circles pull themselves out of poverty within five years, as we did, and that a quarter need ten years. The other quarter take longer because they have serious health problems, or live in an area where the topsoil has been destroyed, or there's no water for irrigation. Every year, also, some people are hit by a typhoon, a flood, or a terrible drought, as the world's climate continues to become more disastrous. I give thanks to Allah that we have been spared, so far, in Sarishpur.

The other aspect of the Grameen Bank that I haven't mentioned is that we own the bank ourselves. There are no absent shareholders who profit at our expense. When the bank makes a profit, it is returned to us as a dividend. It is such a simple idea, that people can co-operate together to help each other. What if the whole world were organized this way? Why do we have to have businesses that break the laws and corrupt people, paying politicians to write weak environmental and safety regulations so that they can make a bigger profit? We have a much better system here. We think about the welfare of the whole village, including the land, the rivers, and the forest. We help each other to be successful in our businesses, and we prosper together. And I am so happy that my grandchildren and great-grandchildren will not have to starve, or prostitute themselves, as I did.

That's why I say a prayer for Muhammad Yunus every morning.

Notes

Nurjahan's life is based on the imaginary life of a Bangladeshi villager. The details about the Grameen Bank are all real, but I have invented the partnership with the Japanese corporation Sanyota, and the part about hydrogen powered vehicles. The description of Mongrando trying to persuade the Grameen Bank to buy genetically modified seeds reflects a real-life episode when Monsanto tried to do exactly that. The section about Mongrando and water is accurate, too — Monsanto is currently buying its way into the water infrastructures of India and Bangladesh. ("Monsanto estimates that providing safe water is a several billion dollar market. It is growing at twenty-five to thirty percent in rural communities and is estimated to be $300 million by the year 2000 in India and Mexico. This is the amount currently spent by NGOs for water development projects and local government water supply schemes and Monsanto hopes to tap these public finances for providing water to rural communities and converting water supply into market." — Vandana Shiva).

I am the English author who wrote the lines about the Grameen Bank being "the single most important social invention of the twentieth century", in my book *After the Crash: The Emergence of the Rainbow Economy* (Greenprint, 1988, 1996). I still believe this to be so.

The data about the world's poorest being reached by micro-lending is correct. The Micro-credit Summit's campaign "Countdown 2005" aims to bring micro-credit to one hundred million of the world's poorest families by 2005, and to 1.3 billion by 2025. The descriptions of poverty come from *Needless Hunger: Voices from a Bangladesh Village* by Betsy Hartmann and James Boyce (Institute for Food and Development Policy, 1982).

For more information:

- Microcredit Summit, 440 First Street NW, Suite 460, Washington, DC 20001, USA; (202) 637•9600; microcredit@igc.org; **www.microcreditsummit.org**
- Grameen Foundation, 1709 New York Avenue NW, Suite 101, Washington DC 20006, USA; (202) 628•3560; info@grameenfoundation.org
- Grameen Bank, Mirpur-Two, Dhaka, 1216 Bangladesh; **www.grameen-info.org/grameen/index.html**

earthfuture

This is a story, but it is not a fantasy. We *can* eliminate poverty from the world, if we work together to achieve that goal. My thanks to the staff at the Grameen Foundation for their help in checking this story.

The Groups of Five

Edmonton, Alberta
November 2013

It is quiet now on the suburban street where we live. The children are asleep; my husband, Ben, knows that I will be late to bed; and outside, it has started snowing again. Miguel, the Chilean student who lives with us, is staying out overnight with his girlfriend.

This is my time to compose my mind and, while Chopin's nocturnes make love to my soul, to write my letters. On the other side of the city, my friend Edith is doing the same, sharing a pledge of loyalty we made thirteen years ago. There were five of us then, at the beginning of the new millennium, and there are five of us today — although Edith and I are the only ones from the original group.

> The Right Honorable Marie-Anne Roulleau
> Minister for Foreign Affairs
> House of Commons
> Ottawa, Ontario, K1A 0A6
>
> Dear Marie-Anne,
> I am writing to you from Edmonton, late on a snowy November night. I hope you are well. I want to share with you my hope that Canada will express its support for the motion that is coming before the United Nations People's Assembly next month, to endorse the proposed International Treaty for the Protection of the Earth's Aboriginal People. As you know…"

I always try to make my letters personal and to avoid sounding judgmental or angry — that was part of the agreement we made when we set up our Group of Five, all those years ago. There were so many things going wrong in the world at the time — it felt as if the planet's social and ecological cohesion was unraveling. We wanted to do something that would make a difference, that would enable us to feel better about the world that we were passing on to our children. And though I'm slightly ashamed to admit it, we wanted to do so without turning our lives upside down.

It was January 6th, 2000, when we first met and established our Group of Five. I was twenty-five years old at the time, and we saw the group as our birthday gift to the new millennium. It wasn't a spontaneous gesture of political activism. We had thought about it extensively, researching similar initiatives. There was Amnesty International, which used personal letter-writing campaigns to great effect to free political prisoners around the world. There was an organization called 20/20 Vision, which sent its members a monthly briefing on a social or environmental issue of importance, asking them to write a personal letter to the relevant minister. And there was an organization called RESULTS, which consisted of small groups of people working to eliminate world hunger, who wrote letters, submitted opinion pieces to the papers, and arranged one-to-one meetings with their politicians. By being polite, well-researched and very focused, they achieved some remarkable results — that's where they got their name.

We decided that whatever the issue we chose to focus on, we would follow seven principles: (1) we would research our subject material thoroughly, so that we were properly informed; (2) we would choose goals and objectives that were clear and achievable; (3) we would seek win-win solutions that would bring people together, not divide them; (4) we would build personal relationships with the people we wrote to; (5) we would use the letter columns and opinion pages of the world's newspapers and the Internet to share our ideas; (6) we would enroll supporters who would write e-mails for the causes we were fighting for; and (7) we would be kind to each other and remember to have fun. Marjorie called it the Fourth Law of Sustainability: "If it's not fun, it's not sustainable."

Our first goal was also our biggest: a Global Treaty on the Abolition of

Nuclear Weapons. It was unthinkable that as a global society, we should be building and maintaining nuclear weapons. If they were ever used, the subsequent nuclear winter would mean the probable death of all living things, except a few algae, and organisms that could survive in the dark. How could we even *contemplate* having such weapons?

We knew there was a well-organized global movement pursuing the elimination of nuclear weapons, which made it easier to adopt as a cause. We decided that our best contribution would be to persuade Canada to adopt an active leadership role, making the treaty a key objective of Canadian foreign policy, and then working with other countries to get the treaty adopted and ratified by the United Nations.

We wrote to every Member of Parliament in Ottawa, and chose thirty-five who responded, including MPs from each political party. We then went to Ottawa to meet them and adopted seven each, writing to them each on a monthly basis, giving them the latest news.

It makes it sound so easy when I say it like that. Encouraged by their response, we used our personal connections to establish a second Group of Five in Winnipeg, who adopted another thirty-five MPs, bringing the total to seventy. Using e-mail, we kept abreast of global developments and developed ties with other groups that were campaigning for a treaty, such as the World Federalists, and Physicians for Global Survival. Meanwhile, we were quietly collecting the e-mail addresses of people who supported what we were doing.

When the issue came before cabinet for discussion, we organized a mass e-mailing to every minister, and submitted opinion pieces to most of Canada's newspapers, forwarding every article which appeared to our MPs. Afterwards, when the government had agreed to adopt the treaty as a major foreign policy objective, we took the time to write to each MP, thanking them personally for their efforts. We always made a point of treating the MPs as we would a friend — never as enemies. If there was one thing that was preventing people from achieving political results in those days, it was their hostility to their own leaders. The media were always looking for politicians to attack, which encouraged a cynical attitude.

Our next step was a big one, which we did not undertake lightly. We decided to organize Groups of Five in every country in the world — ordinary people, like us, who would adopt their members of parliament, congressmen and other representatives, and feed them information, giving them the support they needed to advance the cause of a global treaty. We knew that the world's nuclear powers (the United States, Russia, India, Pakistan, China, Israel, Syria, Saudi Arabia, Britain and France) would be the biggest obstacles, but we couldn't let that stop us. It was our children and our grandchildren we were thinking of, not the complexities of the world's regional conflicts.

We could never have established those groups without the use of the Internet. Once we started asking, describing the limited nature of the commitment that the Groups of Five involved, people started picking up our request and bouncing it to friends and e-mail lists all over the world, translating it as they went. Within a year, we had Groups in a fifth of the world's nations, including all the major powers. The rest took longer. For some of the smaller nations such as Sierra Leone and Rwanda, where people were more preoccupied with survival than global activism, we never succeeded.

We encouraged each Group of Five to establish sufficient Groups in each country to make personal contact with a fifth of the federal or national politicians — enough to create a critical mass. In India, that meant establishing thirty Groups. Working through the Indian peace movement, they quickly met their target, but the Indian and Pakistani Groups had an additional challenge: they had to persuade their governments to start talking on a regular basis, and to make a commitment that neither would be the first to use nuclear weapons. Once that was in place, and once China had agreed to a similar commitment, it was easier to discuss eliminating nuclear weapons altogether. Many of us worked overtime then, writing letters of support to the Indian, Pakistani, and Chinese politicians. Knowing their names and having their photos beside us made a difference, since they ceased to be an incomprehensible jumble of names and became individual people, doing their best to serve their countries.

The Global Treaty to Abolish Nuclear Weapons was finally signed in 2009, nine years after we joined the campaign. By then there were 525 Groups of Five in North America, pursuing a variety of goals, some global, some local. Today, in the world as a whole, there are over 7,000 Groups; I've long since stopped keeping track. It feels as if a global brain is developing in which we are the cells, and our many connections are the synapses.

In the wake of this success, we found ourselves being invited to speak at many luncheons, conferences and service clubs. It was the simplicity of our methods that attracted people. We were not experts; we were three ordinary women and two men who happened to have taken on a rather extraordinary task, and who were making progress by taking a manageable approach. The vision was big, but we moved one step at a time, in ways that felt comfortable. The Groups of Five appealed to people because they emphasized personal relationships. You were no longer an anonymous individual in the Canadian prairie or wherever. You were writing to someone you knew, building relationships that could change the world.

Wherever we spoke, we shared our seven basic principles and told people how easy it was to form a Group. With the Treaty achieved, we encouraged new Groups to choose their own goals and embark on new campaigns. It was the politics of the personal, and it worked.

It was the Groups of Five, working alongside groups like Greenpeace and the Sierra Club, that persuaded the world's governments to introduce a global tax on the oceans and the atmosphere (the global commons), with the proceeds being used to police the oceans against overfishing and the illegal use of driftnets, and to reduce the global emission of greenhouse gases.

Similarly, it was Groups of Five that did the legwork and persuaded the world's politicians to endorse the Global Sustainable Trade and Environment Agreement (GSTEA), placing social and environmental protection ahead of simple profit, as a precondition of trade deals between nations. This was a huge campaign that ran into a wall of opposition from the big corporations, the very ones it was designed to control. The best gave us their encouragement and support, but the worst used all sorts of dirty tricks to try to stop the treaty.

The Groups kept on writing, however, feeding examples of corporate wrongdoing to their political representatives in countries all over the world. Month by month, they built a climate of opinion that was impossible to ignore, laying the political groundwork for the Treaty's eventual success. There were many other groups campaigning for the same goal, but the Groups of Five contributed a vital part.

In the last few years, our work has been enormously assisted by the arrival of electronic tablets and Smart Radio. The tablets have taken over as the main source of news information, and the specialized news services have enabled us to reach millions of people who listed "global activism" or "environmental news" as an interest when they signed onto their news servers.

It has been the same with Smart Radio. My Internet-based Smart Radio searches the station-schedules for programs that interest me, and packages them into a personal listening schedule that suits my listening habits. It makes old-fashioned radio seem positively archaic. Smart Radio has been attracting some very specialized listeners, which has encouraged radio stations to trade programs around the world using the internal radio currency they have set up, the frequency. Last year, we made a one-hour documentary program about our campaign for an International Treaty for the Protection of the Earth's Aboriginal People. It took us seven months to put together, but it cost us less than $1,000, and we were able to distribute it around the world through Green Radio International, which links progressive radio stations. Like the Internet, Smart Radio is a godsend for democratic activism.

The Internet has also been helpful in establishing the new concept of "democratic transparency," which encourages governments to share not just their press releases but also their actual deliberations, on the Internet, where everyone can follow them and join in. A few months ago, during our

Aboriginal Treaty campaign, we discovered that the Brazilian government had established a committee that was quietly drafting new legislation to govern Brazil's indigenous tribes, which struggle to survive in what's left of the Amazon basin. By exposing this on the Brazilian Smart Radio stations, the Brazilian Groups of Five were able to force their government to open up the process, and involve the tribes in the negotiations. The tribes may seem to live in a very simple manner, but they've got all sorts of wind-up and solar-powered radios and computers these days. Taken together, the Internet, electronic tablets, Smart Radio stations and transparent government are having a tremendous influence on the deepening of democracy around the world.

The last five years have been amazing. Following a campaign started ten years ago by a Group of Five in Lincolnshire, England, the entire United Nations has been re-invigorated through the establishment of the People's Assembly. It is based in a different country every ten years, starting in Costa Rica, and has 1,300 delegates who have all been elected using proportional representation, including China, on the basis of one member for every five million people. With the world's population standing at seven billion, China has 320 seats, and India has 225. The United States has 72 seats and Canada has just 7, but we make our influence felt.

It's thrilling to see this happening, as one more step towards the evolution of a proper global democracy based on the values of sustainability, justice and peace. While we and thousands like us have been slowly persisting with our visions and commitments, the planet has been quietly awakening, blossoming into a new self-confidence. And we've only just begun.

Notes

The Groups of Five do not exist as such, but both RESULTS and 20/20 Vision do. I recommend *Reclaiming our Democracy* by Sam Harris (Camino Books, 1994), a very inspiring book about the RESULTS movement, written by its founder, which explains their methods in detail. It was my personal book of the year in 1997.

Like the electronic tablets, Smart Radio does not yet exist.

For more information:

- 20/20 Vision (USA), 1828 Jefferson Place NW, Washington, DC 20036, USA; (202) 833 • 2020
- 20/20 Vision (Canada), #103, 2609 Westview Drive, North Vancouver, British Columbia, V7N 4N2, Canada; (604) 983 • 2525
- RESULTS (USA), 440 First Street NW, Suite 450, Washington DC 20001, USA; (202) 783 • 7100; results@action.org; **www.action.org**
- RESULTS (Canada) Blaise Salmon, 1320 Bond Street, Victoria, British Columbia, V8S 1C4, Canada; (250) 384 • 1842; bsalmon@canada.com; **www.results-resultats.ca**

Jomo's Death

Nairobi, Kenya
August 2014

Oh Jomo, what are we going to do without you? You, who taught us so much about living, and how to love this crazy world we live in. The simple yellow-washed room where you spent your last few months is quiet and still now, as if you've just slipped out and will be back in a moment. It is filled with your light. We've taken your bed away, but otherwise we've left it just the way it was. The students use it as a kind of sanctuary these days. So do I.

You was only thirty. You could have lived till eighty, if it weren't for this disease that's been killing us. We grew up as boys together, playing like monkeys in the jungle that was the slums of Nairobi, hassling the tourists in the hope of a dollar, running errands for the big market mamas. Our mothers were always chasing after us, calling out for us not to get into trouble, while quietly hoping we'd come back with a big fat mango or a pocketful of rice.

We brought back the mangos; and then we started to chase those other mangos — remember? Remember that shack you found that was empty in the daytimes — how we began to discover what we thought it was to be a man? We had fun, right? The girls did too — they were just as wild as we were. I doubt if any of us was more than fifteen years old.

I sometimes wonder what would have happened if you hadn't got busted, man. I'd probably be some kind of pimp or petty hustler, if I was alive at all — instead of being a teacher at this incredible school you founded. How did that happen, man? Do you know how many people came to your funeral? Fifty thousand — that's how many people the police said lined the streets when they carried you by. You was like royalty, man. Not even Kenyatta got that kind of a send-off.

You should see this place today. It was busy enough before you died — but now? It's just cooking. There's people comin' and people goin' and people doin' almost everything — and there's kids from places as far away as Britain and Italy and Australia, come because they've been inspired by you and what you did. You was something, man. We had a whole bunch from Switzerland here last month, helping fix them solar roofs you loved so much, digging the gardens, volunteering in the clinic. Man, some of them kids got dads so wealthy they could buy the whole of Nairobi if they wanted it. But hey, who'd want it? When they went back, they said they was going to set up a Jomo Malaho Green Village Fund to pay for some of the things we need, like medicines, and reading books for the schools. And you should see the size of the package of condoms we was sent last week. Man, you could do it twenty-four hours a day for a whole year with all them, and never catch a thing. Okay, okay — I know you said to lay off the girls, put my mind to better things. But some days, I feel so good, I wanna do both. You really started something here, Jomo.

You know what I regret the most? It's that you never got to write that book, to tell us all what really happened, that time you got busted. I mean, stealing radios — that's pretty small stuff. They could easily have sent you to jail and you'd a been dead by the time you was twenty. Instead, they sent you to the farm — and you came back changed, started doing all this stuff. What did they do to you out there — dress you up in a halo? But man, it's beautiful, what you started. The way we was living in this hell-hole was like animals, we was so crowded, all the men and women getting sick, getting pregnant, dying, spreading the disease around everywhere. Them politicians and fatcat business types didn't care nothin' for what we was going through in the shantytowns. They just took the aid packages and spent them on them fancy cars and bigger sticks for the police, the better to beat us with.

When you came back from that place three years later, you had us all organized, cleaning the streets, digging the gardens, filling them up with vegetables. You even had us building those "Jomo" vertical gardens, beans and soy and stuff climbing all over everywhere. That was wild! That was a great day when we all went down to the city hall to protest the fact that there wasn't no proper drainage, no clean water, no sewers, where we lived. The way you got them councilors to come out and tour the shantytowns instead of getting angry at them — that was genius, man. You remember their faces when that big mama pulled up her skirt and sat herself down on that composting toilet of hers? They'd never seen nothin' like that. Things started changing round here pretty soon after that. Now we've got composting toilets everywhere, and all that good shit going back onto them beans. You was always telling us how we had to close the loop, and we all kept laughing, saying, "Close the poop! Close the poop!" You had us god-near dead with laughing so much, trying to close the poop.

Man, how we miss you. There's green villages springing up all over Nairobi today. It's the best cure for the disease anyone's found yet. Keep the kids busy with all this community stuff, building toilets, planting gardens, helping their folks with the businesses they're starting, getting the kids into the schools we're busy building, showering them all with condoms — the rate of new infections has been falling every year. There's a lot less messing around going on, from what I gather — but that's only part of it. The kids feel they're part of something, not the tribal stuff our folks used to do, and not the nothing stuff you and I used to do neither, looking out for ourselves in the urban jungle.

And all that community banking stuff you got them to bring in? That's been wild. Them big sky-talking banks won't touch it — they're far too tall at the top of them big towers to see what we need. But we've got banking partners coming in from as far away as Bangladesh and Chicago, helping us set up these community lending circles, making sure people get the credit they need to build their businesses and make a living. And you know that big New York thing you was always going on about? World Bank, or something? It's gone — like closed down. Cosmo said it was far too corrupt to be worth bothering changing. There's some new thing going to replace it, like the "World Earth Bank," he said they was gonna call it. I just hope it's not more of the same old stuff, hiding behind a fancy new name.

Cosmo says they're talking about posting every loan they propose making on the Internet where we can see it for ourselves, and like they won't approve it unless it wins support from the community it's supposed to go to. Cosmo's smart that way — and there's him living in that tiny house with his mango trees, up at 6 am every morning, doing stuff on the Internet, joining in those big conferences, talking to Green Village people all over the world.

Did you hear that, man? Like, "all over the world." Yeah — those were the words. This isn't just little old us in noplace Nairobi no more. Cosmo says there's Green Villages jumping up all over the place, places I've never heard of, like Bolivia, and Orissa. I mean, I don't want you to get big-headed about this, but man, you really started something when you came back from that farm place with your talk about working with the spirit of nature, and building our lives from the heart up. You showed me how to stop being angry all the time — that was the first time anyone done that. Man — was I angry? I was angry at everything. You showed me how I was being a stupid pretty boy, using my anger to show myself off, win attention. First time anyone told me that — showed me a mirror, like. You told me how you'd been so angry too, how they'd given you all those things to smash until it just felt so stupid. "Anger is simply the frustration of a beautiful soul," you said they'd told you — and then they'd shown you this amazing thing, how every single one of them had felt the same kind of anger, and how they'd given you your own special headband to wear when you was angry — until it was all you could do to stop laughing at yourself. "OK," you said then. "If I can't do angry, what can I do?" "Change the world, man," that's what they said. "Change the world." And how you was a beautiful being, how we was all part of this beautiful thing called life, and what a shame it was to waste it.

Then you came back, and you had us in them "Remembering the Spirit" groups you set up. You remember that? Of course you do. That just did something, man. There was so many of us feeling angry, or mad, or just plain hopeless. And so many dying. Every week we was sending someone's ashes back to their villages to be scattered. It's hard to change the world, or feel good about yourself, when there's so much dying going on. We really needed something — but we thought it was medicines. We didn't know it was medicines plus fresh food plus something to believe in. Man, how I love you. You spent ten years wasting away in front of us, and all that time you inspired us to go out and get ourselves organized. If it hadn't been for you, I'd be dead today. I'm just so glad you met Wangari before you died. And Jomo? We've got this fantastic little girl now. And yes — she's just fine.

I've got to go, Jomo — they're calling me to come and help cook supper. I know they say you've left us, but I know they're wrong. You never left us, Jomo. You's here in every brick you helped us lay, every garden you got us to build, every heart you filled with self-belief. You never left us. Most of the kids know that. But I sure do wish you was still around to sing and laugh with us, to see how all these villages is doing, to see this beautiful new Africa that's emerging from the ruins. They said we was a write-off, them fancy American journalists. Now who's laughing? Man, we're so proud of you, Jomo.

Your friend, Julius Onyango

From Jomo's obituary in the *Times of Kenya*, June 3ʳᵈ, 2014

Jomo Malaho died on May 30th, 2014, at the age of 30, after a ten-year struggle with AIDS. Following a delinquent childhood in the slums of Nairobi, Jomo was arrested for theft and sent to a Rediscovery Youth Camp out in the bush, where he spent three years confronting his fear and anger, learning to transform his demons, listening to the elders, and learning some of the skills that he would need to build a more sustainable future for his people. When he returned to Nairobi in 2002 he established the non-profit "Green Villages of Hope," and started to attract young people to work with him. Today, there are fifteen Green Villages in Nairobi, and another 133 villages spread throughout urban Africa and around the world. Studies have shown that the rate of AIDS infection among young people in Green Villages which have been established for three years or more has fallen by 50 percent and is continuing to fall, offering the hope that the disease might be defeated more quickly than had previously been thought possible. Jomo left no close family. His mother, father and two sisters all died from AIDS. He left a massive following of youth, however, who are continuing the work he started. His name will be forever praised among people old and young, in the urban neighborhoods of southern Africa and around the world.

Notes

"Spurred by poverty and lack of widespread prevention efforts, the AIDS virus continues to rake across sub-Saharan Africa — where seven of ten global HIV infections and nine of ten global AIDS deaths occur. In a dozen African nations, at least tenpercent of the adult population carries the virus." (*Vital Signs* 1999, Worldwatch Institute, New York)

Julius would have been thinking to himself in Swahili, not in this kind of "street" English.

For These Things, We Are Grateful

For our bodies, that give us life;
for our friends, who give us love.
For the myriad creatures, plants and trees
who make this world such a joy.
For the chance to work and follow our dreams,
and for the rewards of effort and success.
For the anger, that lets us rage;
for the tears, that let us weep.
For the mystery, that lets us heal;
for the happiness, that lets us laugh.
For the future, that lets us hope;
for the past, that lets us remember.
For our ancestors, who gave us what we have, and
for our children, who will inherit what we leave.
For the Earth, that gives us life,
and for the Great Being, who gives us all.

For these things, we are grateful.

The Earth Pledge

The Earth Flag is my symbol
of the task before us all.
We are the custodians of the future of the Earth.
Unless we check the rapacious exploitations
of our Earth and protect it,
we have endangered the future of our children
and our children's children.
It reminds us how helpless this planet is —
something that we must hold in our arms
and care for.

Margaret Mead, March 1977

I THEREFORE PLEDGE to live, work and act in a loving, respectful way towards this Earth that I call home, and towards all who live upon it, every insect, animal, fish, bird, plant, human and tree. In honor of this pledge, I commit myself to the following:

- TO LIVE simply, resisting the urge to overpurchase, and avoiding the purchase of things produced which I know have involved social or environmental harm.
- TO EAT wholesome food produced locally by organic methods, and to minimize my consumption of food which I know have involved cruelty to animals, or other environmental harm.
- TO CONDUCT myself in a harmonious, peaceable manner, avoiding selfish or arrogant behavior, sharing love and kindness with those around me.
- TO TRAVEL where possible by foot, bike, skate, transit, train or carpool, and to minimize my use of fossil-fuel-powered vehicles,

minimizing my contribution to global warming and air pollution.

- TO WORK at an activity which brings me fulfillment, and which contributes to the well-being and harmony of the Earth, and its many people, plants and creatures.
- TO INVEST any savings that I have in a socially responsible manner, supporting projects and businesses that benefit nature and humanity.
- TO AVOID the use of chemical drugs, pesticides, fertilizers or cleaning products which are harmful to human, animal or plant life, and to use instead natural alternatives which have been created for this purpose.
- TO STUDY the details of issues that attract me, so that I can act in a useful, well-informed manner, and make a valuable contribution in my chosen field.
- TO EXPLORE the realities of people and ecosystems outside my homeland, that I may better understand their hopes and difficulties.
- TO PROTEST those activities which I consider harmful to the present and future well-being of the Earth, and its many people, plants and creatures.
- TO SUPPORT those who are working for the well-being of humanity and the Earth and to vote for those who step forward represent my hopes.
- TO JOIN with others who are working for similar goals, contributing my gifts, enjoying the gifts that come with fellowship, and fulfilling the dream of the Earth.

SIGNED	WITNESSED

NAME	DATE

...something that we must hold in our arms and care for.

And If

And if,
amid our strivings
and our rushing lives
we find for just a little while a place of peace
where hope is more than just a dream,
then should we all take heart
and understand that we shall all yet see
in days to come, in years unfolding
the brilliant dawns of love
awaiting us.

About the Author

GUY DAUNCEY is an author, speaker, organizer and consultant who specializes in developing a positive vision of a post-industrial, environmentally sustainable future, and translating that vision into action. He has been self-employed for the past twenty-five years, working in the fields of positive social, economic and environmental change in Britain and Canada.

He has traveled to twenty-five countries, and co-established a number of initiatives including the British Unemployment Resource Network, the UK Education for Enterprise Network, the UK Social Investment Forum, EcoNews, the Victoria Green Pages, the Victoria Car Share Co-operative, and the Street Volunteers. His passion lies in creating a positive vision for the future, and showing how it can be implemented in practical ways. He is presently engaged in work to establish a car-free ecovillage on the coast of British Columbia, and in founding and directing a new organization — The Street Volunteers — which will draw neighbors together on the streets and in the apartments where they live. He is also involved in promoting solutions to global climate change through a Canadian Broadcasting Corporation (CBC) film, *Turning Down the Heat*, its website, and a future book.

Previous publications include *After the Crash: The Emergence of the Rainbow Economy*, (Greenprint, UK: 1988) — awarded the Green Book of the Year award in Britain, 1988; *The Unemployment Handbook* (NEC, UK: 1981); *Nice Work if You Can Get it — How to be Positive About Unemployment* (NEC, UK: 1983). And several books for schools, including *Earthcrisis* (Hobsons, UK: 1988); *Training, Unemployment, and the Meaning of Life* (Hobsons, 1987); *Relationships* (Hobsons, UK: 1988).

New Society Publishers' mission is to publish books that contribute in fundamental ways to building an ecologically sustainable and just society, and to do so with the least possible impact on the environment in a manner that models that vision.

If you have enjoyed *Earth Future: Stories from a Sustainable World,* you may also want to check out our other titles in the following categories:

Progressive Leadership
Ecological Design & Planning
Environment & Justice
New Forestry
Accountable Economics
Conscientious Commerce
Resistance & Community
Educational & Parenting Resources

For a full list of NSP's titles, please call **1•800•567•6772**
or check out our web site at:
www.newsociety.com

New Society Publishers